Happy Event

A Comedy

Richard Everett

Samuel French – London
New York – Sydney – Toronto – Hollywood

CHARACTERS

Jane Harbottle
Peter Harbottle
Stella
Mike
Polly
Grigore

The action takes place one evening in the living-room of Peter's and Jane's house

Time—the present

ACT I*

The living-room of Peter and Jane Harbottle's house in New Malden, Surrey.

It is early evening. The room is open plan. It has a door upstage and facing us which leads to the kitchen off. Nearby is a hatch with double doors also leading to the kitchen. Downstage is a doorway which leads to the hall and front door. We can see the beginnings of the stairs going up. We cannot see the front door itself. There are patio doors in the living-room and evidence of a garden outside. The living-room is tastefully furnished, Habitat-style, but no obvious signs of wealth. The Harbottles have created a warm, pleasant atmosphere in a fairly typical suburban home. Downstage is a sofa with cushions and coffee table with a couple of easy chairs. Upstage and near the hatch is a dining-table. Near the door to the hall is a telephone on a small table and, next to it a sideboard. Also in the room is a combined record and cassette player

Stella enters from the kitchen with a mug of tea

Stella Well frankly, Jane—I couldn't be more delighted. I don't know why you're in such a state.

Jane enters at speed with a table-cloth and cutlery. She is on edge

Jane I'm not in a state. (*She puts the cutlery on a chair and wrestles with the table-cloth, trying to spread it*)
Stella Peter will be thrilled.
Jane I don't think so.
Stella He'll be over the moon.
Jane I don't think so.
Stella You're becoming parents, Jane!
Jane We didn't plan it, Stella!
Stella Giving him his first child!
Jane It's one too many.

Jane dumps the cutlery on the table and exits briskly to the kitchen

Stella (*calling to her*) Oh, for goodness sake! He's becoming a father. He'll be straight down the sports shop and buying goal posts!

Jane opens the hatch and looks through

Jane Yes! And dribbling me up the garden! (*She puts things in the hatch*)
Stella Why are you being so negative?
Jane His career Stella! It's really taking off now.

---

*N.B. Paragraph 3 on page ii of this Acting Edition regarding photocopying and video-recording should be carefully read.

Stella Excellent. Nothing like a pooey nappy to bring him down to earth!

Jane re-enters

Jane Look. This posting in Saudi Arabia. He was offered it because he had the right qualifications and NO family ties. With me pregnant, they'll give it to someone else and Peter's going to be heartbroken.

Stella But this is a once-in-a-lifetime thing, Jane! Postings abroad are two a penny these days.

Jane (*taking things off the hatch to the table*) They're not, Stella.

Stella They've got other branches, haven't they?

Jane Fishguard and Iceland. And you don't get a swimming pool and servants living in.

Stella Well . . .

Jane It's no use pretending.

Stella He's becoming a dad. He'll be ecstatic.

Jane He won't be ecstatic at all. He'll pour himself a large gin and throw himself through the patio doors.

Stella I don't believe a word of it!

Jane Neither do I. He'll pour himself a large gin and throw *me* through the patio doors.

Stella Why can't you be more positive?

Jane (*sitting at the table*) Because I feel as though I've failed him in some way.

Stella What nonsense! Why?

Jane I'm always letting him down. Even the tiniest things and I always seem to fail him.

Stella Like what?

Jane Like the television licence. Umpteen times he reminded me. It sat on the hall table for a month. The next thing we knew there was a detector van at the door.

Stella But Peter's very patient . . .

Jane Patient? Oh yes. Very. Until the fine dropped through the letter box yesterday morning.

Stella But I don't see . . .

Jane I've never seen him so angry.

Stella Jane . . .

Jane What with that and the razor blades.

Stella Razor blades?

Jane I kept forgetting to buy him some more. He's been shaving in the gents at Waterloo for the past week.

Stella But Jane! You talk as though it were the end of your marriage!

Jane It nearly was. He was propositioned twice.

Jane exits to the kitchen

Stella What has any of this to do with you getting pregnant? You're talking complete gibberish. You'll have a nice quiet evening together and when the moment's right . . . you'll tell him.

Jane looks doubtfully through the hatch and then vanishes

Saudi or no—he'll be a very happy young man. I know it. I'm going to ring him up later and congratulate him.

Jane re-appears at the hatch

Jane No you're not!
Stella Yes I am.
Jane Don't you dare!
Stella If *I* don't, Mike will.
Jane No Stella!

Jane vanishes from the hatch

Stella I won't be able to stop him. You know what he's like—any excuse for a party. He'll be straight round here with a bottle of champagne.

Jane enters carrying crockery

Jane Then don't tell him!
Stella Oh, stop panicking woman! Hey, I haven't seen that crockery before. Is it new?
Jane This? No. Old as the hills. Belonged to Peter's grandparents.
Stella It's very pretty. And valuable too, I should think.
Jane Yes. We don't get it out very often. (*She starts laying the table*) Now look, Stella. You must promise me you won't start ringing up. This is a tricky enough operation without you two fooling about in the middle.
Stella I'm not promising anything.
Jane I mean it Stella! If you do ... and I haven't ... and Peter isn't ... and ...
Stella Oh, Jane! Will you stop getting yourself all in a dither about this? You're having a baby. You're going to tell Peter. Peter's going to be thrilled. End of story.
Jane Epilogue: wife found with meat axe lodged in skull.
Stella You're having a child, Jane! It's a wonderful, wonderful thing!
Jane Wonderful, eh?
Stella Absolutely.
Jane You haven't had any.
Stella I prefer aerobics ... and Mike prefers boats. I'm not the pram-pushing sort, Jane. A few years ago—who knows? But we like things the way they are now. Mike does his little surveys, I type out his big reports. Mike collects his big fee ... and I spend it for him. It all works very nicely. Why go and spoil it all by pupping all over the place?
Jane Exactly! That's exactly what Peter will ...!
Stella No! I'm sorry! That was very tactless! I simply meant ...
Jane What?
Stella That Mike and I are very different from you and Peter.
Jane In what way?
Stella Well ... you're younger than me for a start. And Mike's a plodder, set in his ways. But Peter, he's more ... I don't know ... more ...
Jane Flexible?
Stella Precisely.

Jane Yes. I thought you'd say that. Everyone says he's flexible. Flexible Peter and Jolly Jane!

Stella You sound like a blue movie. And besides, Mike's into sailing, not babies. Try asking him to wind a baby, he'd lick his finger, stick it up its behind and tell you it was coming from the south west!

Jane He could learn.

Stella And later on—can you see Mike coping with a neurotic teenager wrestling with acne in the upstairs bathroom?

Jane Not really ... Stella?

Stella What?

Jane They don't all have spots, do they?

Stella Ours would.

Jane So might ours! God, this gets worse by the minute!

Stella Oh, you needn't worry. You've both got lovely skin. Especially Peter.

Jane Especially Peter, what?

Stella Especially Peter's skin. It's like a baby's bottom.

Jane Is it?

Stella Gorgeous. I love it.

Jane Do you?

Stella Don't you?

Jane It's all right. What about Mike?

Stella What about him?

Jane Hasn't he got skin?

Stella Oh yes. Layers of the stuff.

Jane Mike's not fat.

Stella You should see him in the shower. Water cascading off his stomach like a wet duvet!

Jane That's very unkind! He's a lovely man, your husband.

Stella I know. He just hasn't got Peter's skin, that's all.

Jane finishes laying the table and crosses to Stella

Jane You really do find Peter quite attractive, don't you?

Stella He's no Quasimodo.

Jane Yes but, you know ... another time, another place.

Stella Another time, another place, what?

Jane (*teasing her*) Come on, Stella! ... I've seen the way you look at him sometimes.

Stella I don't look at him in any way ... don't be silly ...!

Jane It's all right! It's all right! I don't mind ... it's quite flattering really. I think he finds you quite attractive as well.

Stella Ha! Nonsense.

Jane In fact, I know he does.

Stella How?

Jane He told me.

Stella Absolute rubbish! ... What did he say?

Jane (*going to the sideboard*) Oh nothing ... much.

Stella Come on! What did he say?

Jane Oh damn! My cut-glass candlesticks!

Stella I beg your pardon?

Jane I lent them to Polly. Blast!

Stella Oh. Polly? Who's Polly?

Jane Moved in next door a couple of weeks ago. Mad as a hatter. Little Miss Potty, Peter calls her. I'll have to use these. (*She gets the china candlesticks from the sideboard and a tea towel from a sideboard drawer. She gives the candlesticks a quick polish and leaves the tea towel on the back of a chair*)

Stella Is she the one that keeps bringing back stray men?

Jane That's her.

Stella Yes. I remember you mentioning something. Pushes a library trolley round the local hospital, doesn't she?

Jane (*lining up the candlesticks on the table*) She did. Until someone caught her masquerading as a physiotherapist.

Stella A what?

Jane They found her in the geriatric ward teaching them all break-dancing. Told me today she's applied for drama school — going to be an actress or something.

Stella Grief! So, anyway ... what did he say?

Jane (*putting finishing touches to the table*) Who?

Stella Peter! ... About me!

Jane Oh that. You don't want to know. Why would you want to know?

Stella Because I do. Come on. Out with it.

Jane Well now, let me think. It was something about ... the mature woman and an old fiddle.

Stella You're right. I don't want to know. Heavens, look at the time!

Jane What is it?

Stella Gone seven!

Jane It's not!

Stella I must fly!

Jane I'm coming with you!

Stella No, you're not!

Jane I'll hide in the broom cupboard, then!

Stella Don't be childish!

Jane I know! I'll leave a note!

Stella Oh yes. Good idea: "Dear Peter. Dinner's in the oven and so is a bun. Lots of love, Jane."

Jane I'll say I don't feel well. At least that'll put him in a sympathetic mood.

Stella Now listen. Listen to your old friend. A stiff drink, a big smile — and tell him.

Jane Just like that?

Stella Just like that. The rest of the evening will be a symphony of love and conjugal bliss.

Jane Will it?

Stella Trust me.

Jane I hope you're right.

Stella Believe me. I am. (*She kisses Jane and begins to exit*) Am I right or am I right?

Jane You're right, you're right.
Stella Then smile!

A fixed grin appears on Jane's face

That's better! 'Bye ... Mum!

Stella exits

Jane's face falls. She looks around and gives the table a final check, walking round in a circle

Jane Right ... so. Big smile ... stiff drink. Yes ... Calm. I must be calm. ...

Jane exits to the kitchen as she speaks, then re-enters with confidence, about to practise her speech

The smile. I forgot the smile.

Jane exits and re-enters with an inane smile

Hullo darling! Had a big drink ...! stiff ...! big stiff ...! Oh, knickers!

Jane exits and appears at the hatch

(*In a deep voice*) Hi dad! How's about a shot of red-eye! ... Oh, God! (*She reaches for the electric mixer which is by the hatch. She switches it on, evidently finishing off something she was preparing earlier. We cannot hear her voice but she animatedly attempts her speech in different ways. After a few seconds she switches off and looks at the bowl*) Bluuurgh! (*She lifts the bowl off the mixer stand and paces up and down in the kitchen, beating the contents. She continues to practise her speech*)

Meanwhile the sound of keys turning in the front door is heard

Jane does not register this

Darling, I love you ...

Peter enters, hearing voices from the kitchen. He is about to call out and then stops and listens. He looks puzzled

I love you very much and nothing will ever come between us. It hasn't been easy I know, and perhaps there are better moments than this to tell you what ... I have to tell you. As a sign of our love for one another, as a tribute if you like ... Aaaaaaah!

Jane appears at the hatch and sees Peter standing agog in the living-room. She jumps out of her skin and drops the bowl and its contents on the floor

Jane Peter!
Peter Got it in one.
Jane I didn't hear you come in.
Peter Sorry. The Dagenham Girl Pipers weren't free.
Jane Sit down. Take off your coat.
Peter Wouldn't it be better if I turned my back?
Jane What?
Peter And whoever is in there with you can leave.

Peter exits to the hall to hang up his coat, then re-enters

Jane There's no one in here. Well, there's me of course ... ha!

Peter I heard voices, Jane. Let's not pretend. I don't know who it is—and I don't want to know. Just tell them to go.

Jane Peter. There's no one in here!

Peter I think we can be civilized about this, Jane. Let's try anyway.

Jane See for yourself ... there's no one. Just little me and my friendly old kitchen ... come and look.

Peter I don't want to look. Hearing was enough.

Jane I was talking to myself, Peter. Prattling. You know how I prattle?

Peter I do. And that was not prattle. It was ...

Jane Lines.

Peter Lines?

Jane From a play I'm rehearsing.

Peter What play?

Jane What play?

Peter Yes Jane. What play are you rehearsing?

Jane Oh ... something Stella wants me to get involved with. Silly really. Awfully badly written.

Peter Jane?

Jane Yes darling?

Peter Will you come out of the hatch please?

Jane Oh ... yes, silly me.

Jane comes round into the living-room and puts her arms round Peter

How are you? Had a busy day? You must be exhausted. Would you like a stink?

Peter Pardon?

Jane A stiff drink ... a drink! (*She sits Peter down on the sofa*)

Peter Jane?

Jane Yes, darling?

Peter Are you all right?

Jane Yes. I'll go and get your slippers ... well, no! As a matter of fact, I ... (*She places her hand on her tummy*)

Peter Feel sick?

Jane No ... No. I've got a bit of a migraine actually. Stupid ... think I'll go and lie down.

Peter Now?

Jane Yes. No. Later perhaps.

Peter Right! Let's have it. How did it happen and what's the damage?

Jane What?

Peter The last time you behaved like this you had decided to redesign the car with the aid of a lamppost.

Jane Oh, the car's fine.

Peter The other person's car then? .

Jane What other person?

Peter The other person you hit.

Jane I didn't hit anybody.
Peter Thank goodness for that. Just the car then?
Jane What car?
Peter Jane?
Jane Yes, Peter?
Peter Have you had an accident in the car today?
Jane No, Peter.
Peter Jane?
Jane Yes, Peter?
Peter When I go to the office in the morning I experience an intense sense of forboding at the number of insoluble problems that I am certain will be thrown at me as soon as I walk through the door. In return for taking on this hapless task I am paid a respectable salary. Personally I regard it all as part of life's rich and wonderful pattern. All part of the merry rough and tumble of a working day. However, when I come home . . . something I try and do as often as I can . . . it's really rather . . . nice . . . yes, I think that's the word . . . it's *nice* to know that one isn't going to go through the whole ghastly process all over again.
Jane Yes, darling. I do understand.
Peter Good. I'm glad you understand. It means a lot to me. (*Pause*) Well . . .?
Jane Well what?
Peter What's going on?! Tell me Jane! Before I hurl the sofa through the patio doors!
Jane Aaah! The sofa!
Peter Yes! The sofa! This finely upholstered object that you stick your bum on when you're tired . . .!
Jane The sofa and not me!
Peter The sofa and not you. That is correct. You and the sofa are not the same thing. It is the sofa which will find itself propelled through the patio doors . . .
Jane . . .and not me.
Peter Not you.
Jane Oh, I'm so relieved! (*She throws herself at Peter and pins him on the sofa*) I knew you'd opt for the sofa when it came to it.

Peter is beyond despair

Peter Jane, I think I may be close to tears.
Jane Oh my darling! My poor darling!
Peter What is it? Your mother? Is she coming to see us? Or your brother? He wants to borrow some money? The phone bill? I don't mind how much it is, only . . . only . . . TELL ME!
Jane Nothing! Nothing at all! There's nothing to tell! Nothing's going on! You're here! I'm here! We're both here. Together. And I'm simply looking forward to a quiet evening with you in front of the telly. (*She gets up*)
Peter Then why are you behaving in this peculiar fashion? Why are you so jumpy?

Jane You startled me, that's all.
Peter Nothing more?
Jane Nothing more. Now you just relax and I'll fix us both a drink.
Peter Come here.

Jane goes to Peter, who kisses her

I love you.
Jane I love you too.

They hold each other for a moment. Then Jane speaks, buried in his arms

Peter?
Peter Mmmm?
Jane (*bracing herself but not looking up*) You may have noticed I've made a bit of an effort this evening?
Peter Yes, I meant to say . . . it's nice seeing the old china laid out like that.
Jane Yes. Well . . .
Peter We should do it more often.
Jane I know we should. But . . .
Peter After all, we pay through the nose to have it insured, we may as well use it.
Jane Yes, but can I just explain something . . .?
Peter 'Course you can. What?
Jane Well . . . there's a reason . . . you see . . .

The phone rings

Peter Damn! I'll get it . . . (*Going to the phone*) Pour those drinks, and we'll talk in a minute.
Jane Right . . . (*She makes for the kitchen and suddenly does an about-turn*) . . . Aah! Stella!
Peter (*picking up the phone*) Six-nine-three-oh. Hallo—
Jane (*yanking it out of Peter's hand*) You're too early . . .! Yes! . . . Yes! . . . Yes! . . . Yes! Right!

Jane thrusts the phone at Peter. Peter looks confused

It's for you! David Goodram.
Peter (*taking the phone*) Yes. Hullo David. Sorry about that . . . No, not at all . . .

Jane is hovering about trying to recompose herself

(*To Jane, in a whisper*) . . . Go and get the drinks!

Jane exits

. . . Yes I'm here David. All ears . . . No. Why? . . . To our house, you mean? . . . Well, no. Of course I don't mind . . . I see. Will he have eaten? . . . Oh good . . . Right. OK, fine. (*Laughing*) Oh! You can rely on me . . . (*More smooth laughter*) OK. No problem! Thanks for warning me. 'Bye . . . (*Putting the phone down*) Creep!

Jane re-enters with drinks

Jane Who was that?

Peter Oh, it was ... what do you mean, who was that? It was David Goodram ... you spoke to him, remember?

Jane So I did. Silly me. Ha! Cheers! (*She chinks the glasses together in her hands*)

Peter Cheers ... (*Taking his drink from Jane*) Jane?

Jane What did he want?

Peter What?

Jane David Goodram ... what did he want at this time of day?

Peter Apparently the Greek representative has landed at Heathrow.

Jane So what do we do? Stand up and sing the National Anthem?

Peter Not a bad idea. He's on his way here.

Jane Damn!

Peter What?

Jane Damn good! Damn good show ... I'm delighted. What for?

Peter A communication breakdown.

Jane Well he's come to the right place.

Peter Jane, what ...?

Jane What sort of communication breakdown, exactly?

Peter Oh ... nothing too serious. No one was there to meet him at the airport. He never received his accommodation details and I'm the only one who knows where he's booked into. (*He gets a file out of his briefcase*) David told him to make his way here in a cab.

Jane Is he important, this man?

Peter Grigore? Well ... we don't want to upset him. He's a government representative and the Greeks do all our shipping. But he's on a friendly visit so he only needs jollying along. We have to watch him a bit. He goes a bit wild when he gets to London and he has diplomatic immunity so he can do what the hell he likes. Anyway, David has asked if we can show him some good honest British hospitality ... and cover up a good honest British cock-up.

Jane Will he need feeding?

Peter David said not to worry. He won't stay long ... Come on! It'll be ten minutes chit-chat and out on his ear. We'll still get our quiet evening, I promise.

Jane OK. (*She kisses him and begins to exit*)

Peter Jane?

Jane Yes?

Peter What were you going to tell ...?

The doorbell rings

Jane Can't be him already can it?

Peter Could be. David didn't say how long since he'd phoned.

Jane Well don't bring him in the kitchen. There's egg-white all over the floor!

Peter straightens his tie and turns on a huge smile as he disappears through the hall to open the door

Jane rushes into the kitchen

We hear the door opening

Peter (*off*) Grig ...!

Peter reels back into the room with a girl, Polly, in his arms. She is sobbing

Polly Peter!
Peter Polly! ... Jane?

Jane enters from the kitchen

Jane Peter?
Polly (*rushing into Jane's arms*) Jane!
Jane Polly!
Polly It's Donald!
Peter } (*together*) Who's Donald?
Jane }
Jane Shall I go first or will you?
Peter You. You're better at this kind of thing.
Jane What about Donald? What's he done, Mmmh?

Peter wearily goes to shut the front door

Polly (*barely audible through the tears*) I was only trying to be a little romantic ... candle-lit dinner and everything ...
Jane Yes? ... And what happened Polly? Come and tell us what happened. Here, have a seat.
Polly I'd prepared this lovely meal, all afternoon it took me. Ratatouille and a mixed salad, special pud with whipped cream and a cherry on top ...

Peter re-enters

Jane Sounds gorgeous, Poll! What happened?
Polly He ... he ...
Jane He what? Mmmh?
Polly He ... he ...
Jane Didn't like it?

Polly shakes her head

He'd eaten already?

Polly shakes her head again

What Poll? Tell us in your own time.
Polly He ... He ...
Peter Threw up all over the carpet?
Jane Sssh! Peter!
Peter I can't bear it. The suspense is killing me!
Jane If you can't be sensible leave the room.
Peter He threw it at the wall then?
Jane Peter! For goodness sake!

Peter I've got it! I've got it! He threw it at *you*!

Polly (*howling*) Y-e-e-e-e-e-e-s!

Peter Yes! I knew I was getting close. Should have spotted it much quicker.
That bit of onion in your hair was a dead giveaway!

Jane Peter! Will you get Polly a drink please?

Peter With pleasure ... before or after she has a bath?

Jane Just get the bloody drink will you?!

Peter exits to the kitchen

Now it's all right Polly. Everyone has these little tiffs now and then. It'll
all blow over, you see.

Polly It won't! It won't!

Jane Of course it will.

Polly It won't! ... Babies don't just blow over!

There is a pause

Jane What?

Jeeves-like, Peter returns with a drink

Peter A drink for the lady.

Jane Ummm ... Peter?

Peter Right again! You're getting awfully good at this Jane!

Jane Why don't you go and check the casserole?

Peter The casserole.

Jane Yes.

Peter Well ... I was rather hoping to get the next instalment of this exciting
little drama which has wandered into our lives ... but then again we know
what's going to happen in the end, don't we?

As Peter speaks, Jane escorts him into the kitchen and closes the door

Jane Polly? ... Polly darling? ... Will you repeat what you just said?

Polly I didn't say anything.

Jane Just now ... something about a ... baby!

Polly How did you know!? How could you have possibly known!

Jane You just told me.

Polly Did I? ... Oh Jane! What am I going to do?

Jane Does Donald know?

Polly nods

Is that why he threw the meal at you?

Polly nods

Now Polly, are you sure?

Polly (*thinking hard*) Well ... he wouldn't have thrown it at me for any
other reason.

Jane No! I mean ... are you sure you're pregnant?

Polly Oh! Pretty sure.

Jane Have you seen a doctor?

Polly Not yet.

Jane Well you can't be sure until you've seen a doctor, Poll. How late is it?

Polly I don't know. Getting on for eight o'clock ... Oh, I see! About three weeks.

Jane Well that's nothing!

Peter re-enters

Peter The casserole, you will be pleased to hear, is alive and well and kicking in the oven.

Polly breaks down again

Oh dear, have I said something?

Jane Peter will you just leave us for a few more minutes. This is women's talk.

Peter Oh ... all right. (*He starts to go*)

Polly No. It doesn't matter. I don't mind if Peter hears.

Peter returns

Jane Yes you do.

Peter starts to go again

Polly I don't ... *really.*

Peter returns again

Jane You do Polly.

Peter She doesn't! She's just said she doesn't!

Jane Peter! Will you please leave us alone!

Peter I always miss the best bits. Other people's drama are ... Aah!

Jane pushes Peter into the kitchen and slams the door

Jane Now then Polly ...

Peter opens the hatch

Peter Make it quick you two! We've got this Greek turning up. Ow!

Jane slams the hatch in Peter's face

Jane Now then Polly. Let's be practical about this. You can't be sure you're pregnant.

Polly I am! I know I am!

Jane Three weeks late doesn't mean a thing.

Polly I can feel it, Jane. You wouldn't understand yet but you feel different ... inside!

Jane As a matter of fact I do understand. I happen to know quite a bit about getting pregnant and ...

Polly Oh Jane ... you're not!

Jane What? Well ...

Polly You are, aren't you? I can see it in your eyes!

Jane It's a bit lower down actually, Polly, in my tummy. But ...

Polly Jane, that's wonderful!

Jane Yes, but you see the thing is ...

Polly That makes all the difference!

Jane Polly! Shush a minute!

Polly We'll be going through it together! We'll do exercises and things and have beds in the same ward ... Oh Jane! ... I'm really happy now!

Jane Polly listen ...

Polly I'm so happy! ... I could! Oooh!

Jane Polly! Keep your voice down!

Polly I could cry! It's all meant to be, I know it is!

Jane Polly!

Polly I bet Peter's pleased ...

Jane Well he ...

Polly I must give him a hug. Where is he?

Jane Polly, sit down!

Polly Peter!

Peter (*off*) Hallo?

Jane Polly!

Polly I want to give you a hug!

Jane SHUT UP, POLLY!

Peter sticks his head through the hatch doors

Peter Oh Good. Just what I need ... Aaaaaaargh!

Peter disappears beneath the hatch in the kitchen. He reappears with a contorted face

Jane Darling! Are you all right?

Peter There's stuff all over the floor in here ... I slipped ...

Jane Thank God for that!

Peter Ow! Oh! I've done something to my ankle ... Ah!

Jane Let me have a look.

Jane goes into the kitchen

Polly Is it serious?

Peter Not very. My foot's pointing the wrong way, that's all ... Ah!

The phone rings

Jane comes out of the kitchen, supporting Peter who hops on one leg

Jane Damn!

Polly comes to help Peter

Polly You get it. I'll look at Peter's ankle. (*She grabs Peter's foot*)

Jane (*grabbing it back*) No. You get it. I'll look at the ankle.

Polly But if I look at the ankle you can get rid of whoever it is on the phone. (*She grabs Peter's foot again*)

Jane *You* get rid of them! I belong with my husband's ankle!

Polly What shall I say?

Peter Will somebody please get the bloody phone!

Jane Get it Polly!

Polly obeys. Peter hobbles on to a chair. Jane helps

Peter There's stuff all over the floor in there!
Jane It's egg-white. I did tell you!
Polly Six-nine-three-oh? Hallo? (*To Jane*) It's pips ...!
Jane Pips who?
Polly Phone pips, a coin box ... six-nine-three-oh ... Yes? Yes it is ... Well
he's not here at the moment ... NOT HERE! ... Ah I see. Hold on,
would you? ... HOLD ON! (*To Peter*) It's for you Peter! Sounds foreign.
Peter See if you can take a message!
Polly Can I take a message? ... *Une MESSAGE!* ... No, he's not having a
massage ... A MESSAGE, ME-TAKE-MESSAGEY! Peter this is hope-
less! He thinks he's onto a sauna thingy ...
Peter Here, give that to me. It's probably the Greek ... ow! Damn and
blast! ... (*All smiles and bonhomie down the phone, he speaks in pidgin
English*) ... Grigore ...!

*As Peter takes over the phone and talks to Grigore, Jane takes Polly to one
side and the following dialogue takes place in urgent whispers*

Jane He doesn't know.
Polly Who doesn't?
Jane Peter doesn't.
Polly Peter doesn't?
Jane No.
Polly Oh. (*Pause*) Peter doesn't
know what?
Jane About the baby.
Polly Well of course he doesn't.
You were at great pains to send
him out of the room!
Jane Not your baby ... mine!
Polly Yours? ... Oh *yours*!
Jane Peter doesn't know yet.
Polly Right. Got you. Why not?
Jane I haven't told him.
Polly Well, he's not likely to find
out any other way, is he, silly!
(*Suddenly very serious*) Now Jane.
Listen to me.
Jane What?
Polly You really ought to tell him,
you know! After all, he's bound
to find out sooner or later!
Jane Of course he is! Look Polly,
just watch what you say that's all.
Polly OK. Mum's the word ... I
shouldn't have said that. I think
I'm going to cry again!
Jane Anything's better than putting
your foot in it.

Peter We expect you, yes ...?
... Yes! Yes ...
Is good. ...
Where are you ...?

OK. No problem.
You tell your driver *not* Keyhole
Club, it's Key Hill Drive ...
twenty three ...
New Malden. Yes! ...
That's it! ... OK. ...
and my wife she make lovely
party for you
when you come! ...
... Ha! But of course!
You come quick, Yes? ...

Quick! ... Yes! OK. ... Soon you
arrive ... 'Bye! ... 'Bye!

Peter Stupid wop! Aaargh! Oh, that hurts!

Jane Poor darling! Sit down. Here let me give you a hand.

Peter OK, OK ... don't fuss!

Jane I'm not fussing.

Peter You are. Oh, hallo Polly. You still here?

Jane She's just going.

Peter Oh good.

Jane Peter!

Peter I mean good that you've sorted out whatever it was that needed sorting out.

Polly Is it broken, d'you think? (*Seizing the ankle*)

Peter Aah! ... Not yet.

Jane No ... Just a sprain, I expect. There should be a bandage in the drawer there. Could you get it, Polly?

Polly (*getting the bandage*) Perhaps you should take him to the hospital, Jane.

Peter No thanks.

Jane He hates hospitals. Won't go near them.

Polly Oh you'll have to get used to that, Peter.

Peter Will I?

Polly Yes ...

Jane It's time you did, is what she is trying to say, wasn't it Poll?

Polly No. I meant he'll have to get over that if you're going to have ...

Jane (*glaring at Polly as she takes the bandage off her*) Thank you Polly.

Polly ... an operation.

Peter Yes, well ... I'm not planning an operation in the immediate future. A lobotomy perhaps, when I'm feeling up to it, but just now a little peace and quiet would do very nicely ... Ow! ... Steady!

Jane Sorry. It needs to be good and tight.

Polly Nasty things ... sprains. My mother sprained her leg when she was carrying me.

Peter What was the matter ... couldn't you walk?

Polly In her tummy, silly!

Peter What was?

Polly Me! I was! She was pregnant!

Peter I see! You mean your mother was pregnant with you when she sprained her leg!

Polly Yes!

Peter Yes, well. I suppose that would explain it.

Polly Explain what?

Peter Why you think with a limp.

Jane (*finishing bandaging*) Right. That should do it. Now Polly, isn't it time you went and faced Donald?

Polly Yes, I must. You're right.

Peter You can borrow a plastic mac if you like.

Jane Ignore him, Polly. Now don't worry about things ... not yet.

Polly No. And anyway, now he's had time to think he may ask me to marry him.

Peter Absolutely! It's what most people do when they've thrown a plate of food at you.
Jane Stop being facetious, Peter.
Peter I'm not. I'm being realistic.
Polly A baby can bring people together sometimes.
Peter It can indeed. What baby?
Jane A general observation, I think. Wasn't it Poll?
Polly Um ... Yes!
Peter No ... Hang on a minute! (*He looks hard at Jane*) Is that what all this is about? (*To Polly*) Are you having a baby, Polly?
Polly Yes.
Jane You don't know yet, Poll.
Polly I don't know yet, but I may be.
Peter You may be.
Polly Having a baby, maybe yes.
Peter (*sarcastically*) Terrific.
Polly I'm sorry Jane. It doesn't matter if he knows about mine does it?
Peter Yours?
Polly Yes.
Peter But *yours* as opposed to who else's?
Jane (*suddenly*) Stella's!
Peter Stella's? Mike and Stella?
Jane Yes.
Peter Having a baby?
Jane Yes ... but you're not supposed to know.
Peter Rubbish! When did you hear?
Jane Today.
Peter Where's the phone ...?

Polly picks up the receiver

Jane No!

Polly slams the receiver down

Peter Mike becoming a Dad? This calls for a celebration ... poor bugger. Hand me the phone someone!
Polly You mustn't Peter! Stella would be awfully upset if you knew.
Peter I didn't know you knew Stella.
Polly I don't ...
Jane Not very well ...
Polly But well enough to know that if she knew you knew, I know she'd be awfully upset.
Peter How do you know Stella? She hasn't involved you in this whatsits-name as well has she?
Jane Yes. Polly's playing Madge.
Peter Madge?
Polly I'm bound to lose.
Peter Lose what? I thought you were doing a play?
Jane We are! "Losing" is a theatrical term for ...

Polly Forgetting lines.
Peter Really. And who's Madge?
Polly She's the one who falls in love with the gamekeeper.
Jane But the gamekeeper isn't interested . . .
Polly Because Madge is terribly rich . . .
Jane And the gamekeeper is terribly poor . . .
Polly And has only got one leg.
Peter Madge has only got one leg?
Polly No! The gamekeeper.
Peter I sympathize.
Jane Yes. Well off you go Polly and see Donald.
Peter If he feels like throwing any more food around, tell him to aim some over the fence—I'm starving!
Jane Crumbs! The casserole!

Jane dashes into the kitchen

Polly 'Bye Peter. Hope the foot gets better.
Peter 'Bye Polly. And don't forget to duck when you walk in the door!

Polly exits

Peter slumps in the sofa

There is a pause

You know something Jane?
Jane (*off*) What?
Peter I'm getting old.
Jane (*off*) Oh no! Don't say it's all dried up and shrivelled!

Jane enters from the kitchen

The casserole. It's ruined.
Peter Never mind. Polly'll be back in a minute with a sherry trifle in her hair.
Jane You are awful to her, you know?
Peter I can't help it. She's stupid.
Jane She's young.
Peter She's the same age as you.
Jane I'm young.
Peter No, you're not. You're old and shrivelled like me.
Jane You're not old and shrivelled. You're just hungry.
Peter Where's her mother these days?
Jane Where's whose mother?
Peter Potty Polly's.
Jane Living with a Texas millionaire in Houston, last I heard.
Peter Oh, very convenient! Typical modern, free-thinking parent, that is!
Jane You're quite old-fashioned at heart, aren't you?
Peter Old-fashioned's got nothing to do with it. If she was *my* daughter, *I* wouldn't let her loose on an unsuspecting world like that. Getting herself pregnant and throwing food at the wall!

Jane Polly didn't throw anything at anyone. What's more she didn't *get* herself pregnant . . . it was an accident. It takes two, you know?

Peter No such thing as an accident these days, contraception is as reliable as it's ever likely to be. No excuse for unwanted children . . . they're merely a product of impatient, irresponsible over-sexed youth . . . or just blind stupidity.

Jane Peter! How can you say . . .?

Peter But listen! Never mind Polly, what about Mike and Stella, eh?

Jane Mike and Stella?

Peter Having a kid!

Jane Oh! . . . oh that.

Peter I mean . . . talk about unexpected, that's a real turn up for the books, that is!

Jane Yes. Isn't it, just . . . I think I'll go and clear up that mess in the kitchen.

Jane exits nervously

Peter chuckles to himself

Peter (*calling through to Jane*) Ha! Poor old Mike! This'll shake him up a bit! Ha! Ha! You wait . . . a year from now he won't know himself! He'll have all the tell-tale signs . . .! The gaunt expression, the hunted look, bloody great suitcases under his eyes! Rusks in his hair, the smell of sick on his jacket and the pungent stench of unemptied nappy buckets when you walk through their front door! Ha! It's hysterical! He'll be joining all those battle-weary dads who wander around Safeways on a Saturday morning. I've seen them . . . terror written across their faces! . . . And Mike's gone and bloody well done it! . . . It's hysterical! Mind you, he's got guts . . . I'll give him that. Poor old sod . . . It's no good, I've gotta ring him! (*He gets up and struggles to the phone*) The man deserves a phone call! . . . Jane? I'm going to ring him! You don't mind do you?

Jane (*off*) Ooooooooooaaaaaaaaarrgh!

The sound of something smashing and then silence. Peter hobbles across the room

Peter Jane? Are you all right?

Jane's head appears through the hatch. She is strangely calm

Jane Yes, thank you.

Peter What was that noise?

Jane What noise?

Peter I heard a terrible noise.

Jane Oh, that terrible noise. That was me.

Peter You?

Jane Yes. Why don't you watch telly or something? I've got some clearing up to do.

Peter The mess on the floor, you mean?

Jane No. The casserole.

Peter Just pour it away, can't you?
Jane No. I have to scrape it off.
Peter Leave it to soak, I should.
Jane I can't soak the wall.
Peter The wall?
Jane Yes. The wall. It's all over the wall.
Peter What is?
Jane The casserole is.
Peter The casserole is all over the wall?
Jane That is correct.
Peter How come?
Jane I put it there.
Peter Why?
Jane I threw it.
Peter What for?
Jane I prefer it to the wallpaper. Off you go. Watch the television. I'll see you later. Goodbye. (*She slams the hatch in his face*)

The doorbell rings

Peter Hell! Grigore! I'd almost forgotten . . .

Peter hops into the hall, straightening his tie and turning on the smile again as he disappears

(*Off*) Grig . . .!

Mike ⎫
Stella ⎬ (*together off, singing Al Jolson-style*) Climb upon my knee, sonny
⎭ boy . . .

Peter (*off*) Mike! Stella!

Mike and Stella enter with black stockings over their heads, eyes, nose and mouths cut out and whitened to look like the Black and White Minstrels. They wear boaters. Peter hobbles in after them

Mike Couldn't wait! Brought the champagne! Where's the lady of the house?
Peter I was about to ring you! Listen, Mike . . . and Stella, dear Stella . . . *I am delighted!* I *really* am!
Stella Oh good! I *knew* you would be!

Peter makes Mike and Stella get down on their hands and knees for an encore

Peter Ssh! Ssh! Jane?

Jane enters

Jane Yes?

Mike ⎫
Stella ⎬ (*singing together*) CLIMB UPON MY KNEE, SONNY BOY!

Jane is paralysed on the spot

Mike Ha! Ha! Janey darling! . . . Give us a hug!

Peter It's Stella that deserves the hug. Stella!

All hug

Jane Stella, I must talk to you.
Mike Afterwards. Ladies' private chats come after the toast.
Peter I agree ... Ow! Damn it!

Mike and Stella pull their masks onto their foreheads

Stella Peter! What have you done to your ankle?
Peter I slipped on something in the kitchen. I'm OK. Jane darling, get some glasses would you?
Jane Yes. Right ...
Stella Sit yourself down, Peter, for goodness sake!
Jane Stella?
Stella Yes?

Jane frantically waves behind Peter's back beckoning Stella into the kitchen

Jane Will you give me a hand, please?
Peter It's only four glasses. Stella's staying here with me ... nurse in residence.

Peter and Stella cuddle up on the sofa. Mike tackles the champagne bottle. Jane is at a loss. She daren't leave the room

Hoping for the best, Jane makes a dash for the kitchen. We hear frantic banging about in the kitchen

Well Mike! Another crew member for the old boat, eh?

Unnoticed by the others Jane sticks her head thruogh the hatch to hear what's being said. Then she disappears again

Mike Yes Pete. A few years ... who knows?
Peter Take the heat off Stella, eh? Someone else to shout at when you're sailing round in circles! Ha!
Mike True, true. Mind you ...

Jane leaps out of the kitchen, with the glasses. Her eyes darting in all directions

Ah! Splendid!

The champagne cork pops. All cheer. Mike pours

You know Pete, kids are a wonderful thing. Some people are cut out to be parents ... Jane, your hand's trembling ...
Jane Is it?
Mike Yes. Too much excitement ... as I was saying, some people are cut out to be parents ... and some people aren't. You, Peter, and you, Jane are definitely cut out for it.
Peter Oh Mike! Now you're getting carried away!
Mike No. I mean it ... Jane?

Jane has attempted to manoeuvre herself out of Peter's eyeline. She has got herself into a ridiculous position and is making huge signs to Mike like cutting her throat, gagging her mouth, flushing the toilet, etc

What *are* you doing?!

Peter looks round

Jane Nothing.
Stella You're not going to be sick are you?
Jane Sick? Me? No! Good heavens no!
Mike So! Glasses charged everyone? I give you ... parenthood!
All PARENTHOOD!

There is a pause while they all drink. Jane's eyes dart nervously round the room to see who is going to do or say what next

Stella Oh Peter! I'm so pleased!

Stella cuddles up to Peter on the sofa

Peter Well I'm pleased you're pleased! We're pleased they're pleased, aren't we darling?
Jane Over the moon about the whole thing.
Mike All in all I'd say it was a very pleasing occasion.
Peter You know, we're really touched that you two should want to share this with us so soon, aren't we Jane?
Jane What?
Peter Touched ... I know I am. You're very touched as well.
Jane Oh yes. I'm very touched.
Mike Good old Janey! Tell me, because I'm dying to know, what was your first thought when you found out?
Peter Oh, that's easy! *I* thought: "Where's the phone? Gotta ring the old bugger up and celebrate!"
Mike I wasn't asking you. I was asking Jane. Your first thought, Jane?
Jane Um ...
Peter She knew before I did anyway. Damn cheek!
Stella Well of course! What did you expect?
Jane Stella ...!
Stella Oh you are silly! You men! Honestly ...
Jane STELLA!!!

The room falls silent at Jane's outburst

Stella Yes Jane?
Jane I must talk to you ... urgently. There's something I must show you in the kitchen.
Peter Jane! Stella doesn't want to hear about all that now!
Stella Yes I do, Peter.
Peter It's only a wall full of casserole.
Stella What is?
Peter What she wants to show in the kitchen. Bit of an upset before you came, that's all.

Stella If Jane wants to show me her wall full of casserole, then I shall see it.
Mike Can I see it too?
Jane No! . . . Yes! By all means! What a good idea!
Peter Oh for goodness sake! This is supposed to be a celebration.
Jane Peter! Stay there!

Jane, Mike and Stella head for the kitchen. As they do, the doorbell rings

Stella Shall I go?
Jane No! You come with me!
Mike But Peter can't . . .
Jane Yes he can. He's expecting a Greek.
Stella A Greek?
Peter It's all right Stella.
Stella What kind of Greek?
Jane A Greek! A Greek! The kind that visits!
Mike Let's hope he's got a decent sense of humus! Ha! Sense of humus! All
  right, please yourselves (*pulling his mask over his face again*) Ow!

Jane grabs Mike by the arm and yanks him into the kitchen

*Peter hobbles wearily into the hall and yet again prepares himself to greet
Grigore, complete with smile and* bon homie. *He disappears in the direction
of the door*

Peter (*off*) Grig . . .!

Polly streaks through into the living-room with sherry trifle on her hair

Oh, God! Jane darling! The pudding's arrived!

Jane enters the living-room followed by Peter

Polly throws herself into Jane's arms sobbing

Jane Polly!
Polly I'm so sorry, Jane! I'm sorry to be such a nuisance.
Jane It's all right! There! SSSShh! Come and sit down.

Jane takes Polly to the sofa

Mike and Stella enter from the kitchen

*Polly looks up and sees Mike and Stella with their Black and White Minstrel
faces*

Polly Aaaah!
Jane It's all right, Poll. This is Mike and Stella.
Stella How do you do.
Peter I thought you knew each other already.
Stella No, I don't think we've met.
Peter Yes, you have . . . rehearsing the play or something . . .
Jane Yes! Yes of course they know each other. How silly! Stella, Mike . . .
  take those ridiculous stockings off and show Polly that it's only you!
  Stella, Polly! (*Nudging Polly hard*) Stella!

Polly Oh! Yes!

Jane ⎫
Polly ⎭ (*together*) Hello Stella!

Jane and Polly wave at Stella

Stella No. You must be confusing me with someone else ...
Jane No she isn't!
Peter Polly's going to be Madge.
Stella Is she? Who is she *now*?
Jane She's Polly!
Mike Who's Madge, then? I'm Mike by the way ...
Peter Madge is the one who falls in love with the one-legged gamekeeper. Isn't that right?
Mike Oh.
Polly Yes. I'm Madge.
Stella But I thought you were Polly?
Jane She is Polly.
Stella I'm awfully confused.
Peter Well you shouldn't be. You're the one that's started it all.
Stella All what?
Peter This amateur dramatic thing.
Mike Amateur dramatics! Excellent idea! I've always thought you should get involved in something like that, Stella!
Stella But I'm not! I hate amateur dramatics!
Jane Oh, Stella! Ha! You see what a good actress she is?
Stella Jane?
Jane Yes?
Stella Nothing. Do you mind if I sit down?
Peter Good idea! Everyone sit down.

There is a pause. Jane wanders around eyeing the others

Well, Polly. How are things at the Front? Been mentioned in dispatches yet? (*He picks a bit of cream out of Jane's hair*) Mmmmmmh! ... Delicious trifle! Get some spoons someone!
Polly He's being such a pig.
Mike Who is?
Peter Donald.
Stella Who's Donald?
Mike Is he the one-legged gamekeeper?
Jane I think I'm going to scream.

The telephone rings. Jane is right next to it. She puts it to her ear

Good evening, this is Jane Harbottle here. Could you hold the line please? ... AAAAAAAAaaaaaaaaaarrrrggh! ... Sorry about that. Who's speaking please? ... Oh yes. One moment ... Darling? It's Grigore.
Peter What on earth is he playing at?
Jane I've no idea.
Peter Is he lost?

Jane I've no idea.

Peter Well ask him.

Jane You ask him. He's your Greek.

Peter Please, Jane. I can't keep getting up with this foot ...

Jane Then try the other one ... or better still, crawl.

Peter You're being awfully unreasonable.

Jane If you don't reach this phone by the time I've counted five, I shall simply hang up. One ... two ...

Peter Oh hell! Help me up someone. (*He begins hobbling to the phone*) Jane?

Jane Yes, darling? Three ... four ...

Peter You're a pain.

Jane Yes, darling.

Peter gets to the phone and begins another crazy conversation with Grigore, who is evidently lost. The conversation which is full of bonhomie *as before, continues in the background*

Mike Madge! I'm so sorry, you haven't got a drink!

Jane She'll have to wait!

Peter (*on the phone*) Please! Please! I can't hear! ... What, Grigore? ...

Jane And her name's Polly!

Peter (*on the phone*) Yes, all right, Grigore ... just put the taxi man on ... (*To the others*) Sorry about this. Excuse me a moment ...

Peter wanders into the hall with the phone

Jane takes Mike by the arm and sits him on the sofa. She has an air of authoritative calm about her, almost menacing

Jane Sit ...! Down! Now then, while Peter is on the phone I want you all to listen very carefully. Don't interrupt, just listen. At this precise moment in time ... and for reasons I shall NOT go into ... my husband, Peter, that's him on the phone over there by the way, is under a number of misapprehensions. One: he believes that it is not me that is having a baby, but you Stella ...

Stella But ...

Jane I said don't interrupt! Two: he believes that Polly ...

Mike Polly being?

Polly Me!

Stella I thought you were Madge?

Jane glares menacingly

Sorry!

Jane He believes that Polly, Stella and I are involved in an amateur dramatic performance of a play. The play is all about Madge who falls in love with a one-legged gamekeeper.

Polly And I'm Madge.

Mike I thought you were Polly ...?

Jane grabs a paper knife and holds it to Mike's throat. The others have to restrain her

Jane So! I would like you to maintain this little charade for a while longer. As soon as Peter is off the phone, you will engage in a limited amount of meaningless chit-chat ... and then leave. Am I making myself clear?

They all nod

Excellent. I should perhaps add that the whole situation is entirely of my own doing ... and I apologize. You will all be forgiven if you never speak to me again ...

All Aah! Jane!

Jane HOWEVER ...! Presuming that none of you is interested in some amateur facial surgery, you will do *exactly* as I say. All right?

All Yes, Jane.

Jane No further questions?

All No, Jane.

Jane Right. Well as Peter is still engaged with his Greek, I suggest you use the time to prepare.

All Yes, Jane.

Jane I shall be in the kitchen if anyone needs me, cleaning the casserole off the walls.

Jane exits

Peter continues in the background

Polly Right. So. You're having a baby, Stella.

Mike And you and Madge are in this amateur thingy ...

Stella *Polly* and me. Not Madge. Madge is the one that's in love with the gamekeeper.

Mike Right. Got it. So ... who am I?

Stella You're *you*!

Mike Oh! I thought I was the gamekeeper.

Polly No. The gamekeeper's in the play. Hey! Do you think Madge is pregnant?

Mike Madge?

Polly Yes.

Stella What does it matter if she is?

Polly Just wondered, that's all. I am, as a matter of fact.

Mike Am what?

Polly Pregnant.

Stella Look. Whether or not Madge is pregnant isn't relevant!

Polly I know that! I mean *I am* ... in real life ... *pregnant*!

Mike Oh.

Polly Donald isn't very pleased.

There is a pause

Mike Who's Donald?

Stella Oh God, I can't bear it! Look you two, let's just be clear about what we're doing: I'm pregnant, she's playing Madge and you're just *you*, Donald ... Mike! ... As if that weren't enough.

Polly Sssshhh! He's coming off the.phone.

Peter comes in from the hall

The room is very still. Mike, Stella and Polly stare at Peter with fixed grins. They are frozen in a tight little line along the sofa. They are all tongue-tied. They smile nervously and inanely at Peter as he hobbles across the room using a golf club as a walking stick

Peter Everything all right?

They all nod

Where's Jane?

They all point to the kitchen

Jane?

Jane belts through from the kitchen

Jane YES! ... My darling?
Peter What are you doing?
Jane Just de-casseroling the kitchen wall, my love.
Peter Oh good. Grigore will be here any time.
Jane Oh good. Get lost again, did he?
Peter Just a little, yes.

There is a pause

Jane Well, I see the party's in full swing now.
Peter Certainly seems to be.

There is a pause

Polly?
Polly (*to Stella in a whisper*) Is that me?
Stella (*urgent whisper*) Yes!
Polly Yes?
Peter Did you know you've still got sherry trifle in your hair?
Polly No.
Peter Oh. Well you have.
Polly Have I?
Peter Yes.
Polly Would you like some?
Peter Pardon?
Polly ... Someone to remove it?
Peter Not particularly. It rather suits you. Don't you agree, Mike? ... Oi! Captain Bird's Eye! I'm talking to you!
Mike Sorry ... yes. Very fetching.

There is a pause. Peter whistles to himself

Peter It's gone awfully quiet in here. I didn't miss anything while I was on the phone, did I?

There is a pause

Nobody's died, have they?

Jane Don't be so morbid, Peter.

Peter We haven't had a close encounter of the third kind or anything?

Jane Don't be silly! Whatever's the matter with you?

Peter Nothing. Nothing's the matter with me at all. It's just that I seem to be sharing the room with an entirely different set of people than I was a few moments ago.

Jane Whatever gives you that idea?

Peter The three stooges on the sofa for a start. Or are they zombies?

Jane Zombies? You're not zombies, are you?

They all shake their heads mechanically

Peter More like clones. Clones of people I once knew ... but now ... inhabited by time-travelling aliens which have descended on London to infect the human race with a deadly disease ... POLLY!

Polly screams

Stella Well, I think we ought to be going.

Peter She spoke! She spoke!

Jane You're just being silly, Peter. Now, I'm sure Stella is feeling tired, aren't you Stella?

Stella Tired? Oh! ... Yes. Yes, I am. Could you help me up please, Mike? ... MIKE?!

Mike What? Oh! Yes ... of course. Right ... stand back everyone! Up we come, darling ... easy does it. That's the way ... Got to be careful now.

Polly Here, let me help.

Peter And me! Give me your hand, Stella.

Stella (*real Madonna stuff*) Thank you. Thank you all ... very much.

Jane despairs in the background. The others gather round Stella, helping her out of the sofa and setting off across the room. It is slow painful progress

Peter Don't crowd! Don't crowd! She needs air. You look a little faint, Stella. You sure you're all right?

Stella I'm fine, really.

Peter I'll open the front door. Let in a breeze.

Peter darts into the hall to open the front door

Once Peter is out of sight, the others break off from their charade for a split second. They all speak at once in urgent whispers

Jane		I said meaningless chit-chat. Not a ruddy three-act drama!
Stella		Jane, this is ridiculous! Why don't you just tell him?
Mike	(*together*)	This is completely out of hand! What the hell are we all doing?
Polly		Do you think he suspects anything? You're being awfully good at this, Stella!

Peter reappears at the door

The others instantly resume their charade. Peter stands in the doorway to the hall, fanning through a breeze

Peter Better now?

Stella Yes, thanks.

Peter This'll put the lid on the am-drams, Stella. Who's going to play your part?

Stella I've no idea. I expect we'll have to call the whole thing off.

Polly No, we won't! We'll get an understudy . . .!

Jane dies quietly in the corner

Peter Of course, Polly! You're right! The show must go on!

Mike No, Stella's right. Call it off.

Stella I think it would be best.

Peter How long before the play opens, Stella?

Polly Days!

Mike Weeks!

Stella Months! Months! Plenty of time to get someone else.

Peter But the fans! All those disappointed fans! I tell you what, Stella . . . You could always have a midwife ready in the wings . . .

Polly Yes! And an ambulance standing by . . .

Peter And your GP at the ready in the orchestra pit! Yes. I can see it all: Stella heroically delivering the last lines of the play between contractions with an oxygen cylinder strapped to her back!

As they have progressed to the doorway in this melodramatic huddle, Peter blocks their exit to the hall threateningly with the golf club

Right! I think that's far enough.

They all freeze

Jane Peter? What are you doing?

Peter No. What are *you* doing, Jane?

Jane I don't know what you mean. Stella and Mike are trying to go home.

Peter Indeed they are.

Jane And you are blocking their way.

Peter Indeed I am.

Jane Why?

Peter Because no one is leaving this room until I have established exactly what it is you're all playing *at*! (*He bangs the back of the chair with the club*)

Polly Peter, don't! You've gone all spooky.

Peter Gone all spooky, have I, Polly? Then tell me more about Madge . . . Do you know your lines yet?

Polly Lines?

Peter Yes, Polly. The lines that Madge has to say in the play.

Polly Oh those lines . . . yes.

Peter Good. Tell me some.

Jane Stop it, Peter!

Polly Tell you some?

Jane Stop it, Polly!

Peter Speak, woman!

Polly Well ... she says ... when she's looking out across the frosted fields on a moonlit night towards the gamekeeper's cottage, she says ... um ... she says ... (*Suddenly looking into Peter's eyes*) See, my love! How the milk-white moon kisses the icicled lips of your home. Would that I could melt those lips ... and moisten your gutters!

Peter Moisten my gutters?!

Polly Yes ... and then she rushes across the frostbitten field towards the cottage ... in only a lace nightgown. (*She rushes melodramatically across the room and jumps on the sofa*)

Jane Yes, all right, Polly. Very good. Now I think ...

Peter Does she? And what then?

Jane Peter, this is absurd.

Polly Then ... as she approaches the cottage ... she begins to hear ... music!

Peter Music?

Polly Yes. Drifting on the cold night air.

Peter Who is?

Polly The music is. ... Tra-la-la! Tra-la-la-la-la!

Peter I see. Go on.

Polly Tra-la-la-la! ... Peering through the frosted window—she has to rub the ice off the pane (*She mimes it*) She sees people ... dancing! She sees Kate, the village gypsy, that's who Stella plays ...

Stella Me ...?

Polly ... dancing to the tune of a merry madrigal.

Jane All right, Polly. That'll do. Satisfied Peter?

Peter No. I'm really into this now. I want to know more.

Jane Well, you can't.

Peter How does the madrigal go, Polly?

Jane Will you please let Mike and Stella through so they can go home?!

Peter All in good time. First I want to hear the madrigal.

Jane Peter! You're just playing games!

Peter Games! Me? Not at all. But ... if you're to become the Sarah Bernhardt of Surbiton, I think I'm entitled to a preview. So, Polly ... set the scene and away you go.

Polly I'd really rather ...

Peter Set the bloody scene, woman ... and SING!

Polly Yes. Right. Stella can be Kate over here ...

Stella No! Polly ... Peter ...

Polly Tie your blouse up above your waist. Now, Mike can be one of the musicians behind Kate ... here, put your funny mask on again ...

Jane Please, Polly, this has gone quite far enough ...

Polly (*unstoppable now*) And you, Jane, you're playing ...

Peter Yes, Jane. What are you playing?

Polly Hermione, the cook.

Jane The what?
Peter The cook.
Polly And you're over here stirring the cauldron over the open log fire. Here, tie this tea towel over your head. That's it, great!

Jane looks defeated and absurd with a tea towel on her head

Peter Can I be the game-keeper? I think I'm right for it and . . . (*Brandishing his bandaged ankle*) I've brought me own costume!
Polly Yes. Sit over there and clap along with us. I'll sing the tune through once and then you can join in. Ready?
Jane No we're not ready at all . . .!

It is too late. Polly beings to sing the madrigal. It is really rather pretty and she has a respectable voice

Polly   Summer is a-coming in! Loud now sing cuckoo!
(*singing*)   Grow a seed and blow with me
                        And spring the woods anew!
                        Sing cuckoo! Sing cuckoo!
                        Cuck-oo!
                        Cuck-oo-oooo!
Peter Oh! It's lovely!
Jane Good. Well, that should give you an idea anyway . . .
Peter SING!

Polly sings again, this time making the others join in. She conducts them into a round. By some miracle the whole thing actually begins to take off. Stella launches herself into a fine and mysterious portrayal of Kate, the Gypsy. She dances around the room brushing up against Peter's leg as she passes. Jane and Mike find themselves doing a country reel as the singing accelerates. Peter claps along from the sofa as he gets more and more into the character of the gamekeeper

  Careful, Stella! Remember your condition!

Stella quickly adapts her performance to include her supposed pregnancy

Everyone manages to project the tension of the situation into the character they play. The result is a strange and manic merriment

  Grigore, who is a large and bearded man, appears in the doorway from the hall. He stands, holding a briefcase and dressed in a suit, unnoticed by the others. He takes in the spectacle, expressionless

Then everyone but Peter sees him. The singing and dancing grind to a halt as the others stare at the towering and serious-looking man. Peter sings on for a few seconds and gradually picks up the others' eyeline and looks round

Peter Sing cuckoo! Sing . . . cuck . . . oo! . . . oo! . . . Oh.
Grigore (*in a rich dark brown voice and heavy accent*) The door was open.
Peter Grigore! Ha! You made it!
Grigore Petro.

Peter Yes. Now let me explain what's happening here . . .
Grigore Petro.
Peter You see, early on this evening . . .
Grigore Petro.
Peter There was a slight misunderstanding and . . .
Grigore PETRO . . . EH?
Peter GRIGORE . . . EH!

A broad grin appears on Grigore's face. He envelops Peter in an embrace, lifting him off the ground and kissing him on both cheeks. Peter fights off a gust of garlic breath

Grigore Ha! You shouldn't haff!
Peter Ha! No. Neither should you.
Grigore I am so late! You wait so long!
Peter Think nothing of it. Would you like a wash?
Grigore (*cheekily*) Petro! You shouldn't haff!
Peter No! Quite! . . . shouldn't haff what?
Grigore Oh! You English! Outside is all reserve but inside . . .
Peter Inside?
Grigore Inside . . . the jolly makers! Make party for Grigore! You and your work-fellows!
Peter What? No!

Grigore reaches for his duty free carrier bag

Grigore Come! See! I have gifts . . . (*Producing two large bottles with a flourish*) For you! *Ouzo!*
Peter Well, that's most generous, thank you . . .
Grigore And now we drink and make luff together!
Peter Pardon?
Grigore Yes! "A drink and a luff", is this how you say?
Peter Oh I see. Yes!
Grigore Bravo!
Peter No!
Grigore But why?
Peter Because you don't . . .
Grigore Off course! You are right. I don't know anyone. First I meet your colleagues.
Peter Absolutely. When we get to the office . . .
Grigore (*seeing Polly*) And who is this pretty womans? Beautiful blonde hair! . . . I luff! (*He strokes Polly's hair and sees something on his hand*) Oh . . . Uurgh! What is this?
Peter A . . . new kind of hairdo. All the rage. Look Grigore . . .
Grigore And how they call you, *rapimo?*
Polly (*a bit taken*) Polly.
Grigore Ah! Pretty Polly! . . . And where you work? (*To Peter*) She is a goddess . . .!
Peter Oh well. No accounting for taste.
Grigore In accounts! Tomorrow I come visit you in Petro's accounts!

(*Reaching into his duty free bag*) Here, my dear! For you! Greek perfume!

Polly (*delighted as she takes the box and reads*) *Aphrodite's Wind*! Thank you! Sounds ... lovely!

Peter Grigore, please ...!

Grigore (*seeing Mike with his mask on, nervously to Peter*) Who is this?

Peter Oh, that's just Mike, Grigore. (*Peter signals to Mike to take his mask off*) ... Just a friend ... ha!

Mike (*seizing the chance to leave*) Jolly nice meeting you! I'll be saying ...

Grigore Hallo! Hallo! ... And what you do?

Mike Me? Oh, this and that ... I sail a lot, you know.

Grigore Aha! The Sales Department!

Jane Oh, for crying out loud!

Peter No, Grigore! No ...!

Grigore It must have been you I spoke with on telephone last day!

Mike What? No, I ...

Grigore Yes! (*Reaching in the duty free bag again*) For you I have something wery special ... (*He takes Mike furtively to one side*) ... Greek cigars! A bit special, eh? Make you a little ... wooh! In the head, yes?!

Mike (*quite unaware that he's handling narcotics*) Well, that's terribly kind ... actually I don't ...

Grigore (*in Mike's ear*) And soon I look forward to go jumpy, jumpy in your club ... eh?

Mike Club? No ...

Grigore Yes! You tell me ... all the waitresses are beautiful, blonde ... and headless! Oh! Ho! Ha! Ha!

Mike Headless?!

Grigore No tops! Ha! Ha! (*To Stella*) And you, my dear, what do you do?

Jane Peter, for God's sake do something!

Peter Grigore! No! Wrong! This is all quite wrong! ... These people ... you see ... I ... they ... you don't quite ...

Jane (*firmly and running out of patience*) Grigore! Before you mistake me for something I am not, let me tell you straight away—I am Jane, Peter's husband!

Peter Wife.

Jane Yes. That too. And ...

Grigore *Enchanté rapimo!* Your house is delight to eyes of shagged out traveller!

Jane Most generous. Now look, these people you see around you, aren't who you think. They just happened to be here when you arrived. Understand? Comprenee?

Grigore But of course! (*He smiles at Jane cheekily*)

Jane Thank heaven for that. Now ...

Grigore lets out a booming laugh and lifts Jane up in the air

Oh my God!

Grigore Oh! ... Oh! Ho! (*Tweaking Jane's cheek*) You naughty little English mistress! You not want spoil Grigore's surprise party? ... OK! ... Come! We make party!

Grigore takes off his jacket to get down to business

Jane Right! That's it! I've had enough.

Jane begins feverishly clearing the dinner table. She stacks the plates noisily to one side

Peter No, Grigore! Jane! I can't hear myself think!
Grigore I teach everyone Greek dance!
Jane This whole evening has been an unmitigated disaster!
Grigore (*rushing to his duty free bag*) First we have music!
Peter We haven't any! No music!
Grigore Yes, music!
Peter Where music?
Grigore Here, music! (*He produces a cassette from the bag*)
Peter God! Music!
Jane I don't need all this!

Jane gathers the four corners of the table cloth and scoops the remaining contents of the table, the cutlery, into it. Grigore sees Mike and Stella trying to sneak off

Grigore (*grabbing them both by the arm*) No! Come! You stay!
Jane (*crossing to the hatch with the bundle*) I wash my hands of the whole thing!
Grigore Petro! I sorry! I late . . .

Jane hurls the bundle through the hatch into the kitchen with a crash

Jane exits to the hall

And your wife is upset!
Peter No, she isn't. She's always like this. Now look . . .
Grigore Come! We dance!
Peter We what?
Grigore We dance!
Peter I think not.
Grigore Yes! (*Pulling Mike and Stella into the room*) Iss good for our souls!
Mike I beg your pardon?
Grigore Our SOULS! Iss good!

Jane re-enters with a vacuum cleaner and starts plugging it in

Where is music machine?
Peter We haven't got one.
Polly Yes, we have!
Peter Yes, we have.
Polly It's over here!
Peter It's over there.
Grigore Ah! Good Polly! Pretty Polly!

Jane switches on the vacuum cleaner and starts attacking everything in sight with it. Grigore switches on the cassette machine and Greek music blares forth

Peter Jane! Will you . . .?

Grigore begins Greek dance instruction with Polly

Grigore! Please! . . . Oh, God . . . Thank you! And goodnight! (*He collapses onto the sofa and buries his head under the cushions*)

Grigore and Polly begin their dancing with hands raised above heads and little skips and jumps. They circle each other and it is all quite charming to begin with but gets more frenetic as time goes on

Mike and Stella try to tell Peter that they are going. Peter waves them away without surfacing

Mike and Stella cross over to Jane who is manically hoovering everything in sight. She is bent right over, in grim determination. She lifts up the pile of dinner plates to vacuum the chair underneath. As an automatic reaction and without really looking what she's doing, Stella relieves Jane of the plates and passes them to Mike. Mike, slightly puzzled at why he has acquired this new-found burden and far more interested in getting out, passes them to an eager Grigore

Grigore Ha! Ha! The plates! Now I show you real Greek dancing!

Grigore gives two plates to Polly and has another two plates for himself. He brandishes them over his head. Polly copies with far less confidence but equal enthusiasm

After much arm waving and shouting over the noise, Mike and Stella have told Jane that they are leaving. None of them has noticed the lethal new development to the dancing

Jane Hang on! I'll see you out!

Jane switches off the hoover. There is relative quiet although the Geek music and Grigore's and Polly's laughter still make quite a row

Stella (*as they go*) It really is very pretty that dinner service.
Mike Looks valuable too!
Jane Oh, it is. We don't get it out very often.

Jane, Stella and Mike exit to the hall. What follows, takes place at lightning speed. They disappear for a brief second. Then . . .

Jane ⎫
Stella ⎬ (*together off*) The plates!
Mike ⎭

Peter suddenly leaps out of the sofa and starts flailing about, pathetically grabbing at plates to no effect. He ends up on the floor, yelling for help

Like a well-drilled SAS team led by Jane, Mike and Stella charge back into the room

Mike and Stella grab the plates and Jane walks behind them piling them up. The pile is passed from one to another and finally back to Jane who makes a bee-line for the kitchen

Grigore thinks the whole thing is a riot and goes in hot pursuit

   Jane and Grigore exit

Like a desperate man, Peter dives across to switch off the music. There is silence ... for a brief moment ... then a yell from Grigore followed by a crash

   Jane pushes the hatch doors open

Jane Here is the News. A priceless set of wedding crockery was saved from an untimely end this evening. However, an unidentified Greek is lying unconscious on the kitchen floor. It would appear he slipped in some egg-white that was spilled here some years ago. Foul play is not suspected. This is Jane Harbottle, News at Ten, New bloody Malden.

Black-out

ACT II

The same. About fifteen minutes later

Grigore is in an armchair with a bandaged foot on the coffee table and a plaster on his head. He is mildly drunk. Peter is on the sofa in his shirt and braces

Mike enters from the kitchen with a tray of drinks. The long cigarillo which Grigore gave him earlier protrudes from his mouth awkwardly

Mike Here we are. A last one of these and then we really must be going.

Peter Well done, Mike ... That's an evil-smelling thing you've got in your mouth. Pooah!

Mike I know. Got ever such an odd taste as well. So ... How's the ankle?

Peter Throbbing a bit. I'll be all right. What news from the kitchen?

Mike (*in a Churchillian voice*) Losses appear to be heavy. The casserole's been blitzed into rubble, the walls are under surprise attack and the floor's been completely wiped out.

Peter And morale?

Mike Running high. Polly's hit the ouzo.

Peter Oh grief. Is that good or bad?

Grigore Ah Polly! Where is my Polly? I need her to sit with me.

Peter Yes all right, Grigore. In a moment. I think you should just sit quietly for a while. How do you feel?

Grigore Iss OK! By morning is no problem.

Peter I sincerely hope so. I don't relish the idea of explaining to David Goodram why you and I are wandering round like a couple of paraplegics.

Grigore Vot?

Peter Para ... Oh never mind.

Mike Shouldn't we whip him down to Casualty? Let them check him over?

Peter He's all right. You're all right, aren't you Grigore?

Grigore Oh. Iss nothink.

Peter That's it. You drink your brandy.

Mike How many has he had?

Peter Three, four ... I dunno. With any luck he'll begin to nod off soon and we can point him in the direction of the spare room.

Grigore So Mike! When we go wiggley-bum in dis club you tell me about?

Mike Oh, for Heaven's sake! Peter, we've got to get this cleared up!

Peter He's confused enough as it is. Leave it. I'll sort it all out tomorrow.

Grigore Tomorrow? We go tomorrow?

Peter He'll take you when you're feeling better, Grigore.

Grigore Suddenly I feel better!

Peter Oh ...! You Greeks! You're all the same. Once in London you think it's all bright lights and bosoms!

Grigore Iss true!

Peter Not quite. There are other things besides headless women!

Grigore Like vot?

Peter Like work.

Grigore Pah! Verk! Iss nossink wissout jolly making. How you say? ... All verk and no jolly making makes Jack a thick man?

Mike Yes ... well. Jack has a wife and mortgage to keep up.

Peter And a family now Mike?

Mike And a ... yes, quite.

Grigore (*to Mike*) You haff babies?

Mike Well ...

Peter Not yet. But coming.

Grigore Your wife is ... how you say? ... stagnant!

Mike Pregnant ... yes.

Grigore Oh wonderful! I luff babies! You, Peter, you must haff babies!

Peter Oh ... well ... soon perhaps. When we get back from Saudi.

Grigore Saudi?

Peter Saudi ... Saudi Arabia! Yes. I've got a two year posting there.

Grigore I heard. But ... er ...

Peter But what?

Grigore Nossink. I must have mistake.

Peter Mistake? About what?

Grigore No, no. Iss nossink. My English is terrible ...

Peter Please Grigore. This evening has been fraught with mistakes. One more isn't going to hurt, believe me.

Grigore Well ... I speak wiss you Mike, last day, yes?

Mike If you insist.

Grigore Yes! I say to gal on phone, "Stick me in se Sales Director, please?" ... and I speak wiss you! You Sales Director, yes?

Peter Yes, yes. You spoke on the phone with the Sales Director yesterday. and ...?

Grigore He tell me sat se new Saudi branch is to be managed by David Goodram!

Peter David Goodram managing the Saudi branch? No, you're mistaken.

Grigore Off course. Sat is vot I say! Iss mistake.

Peter David Goodram *was* going to take it on but he decided to accept an offer from another firm. That's why they offered it to me.

Grigore But Mike ... you tell me on phone sat David Goodram he stay now. He stay and go to Saudi Arabia. Everythink change.

There is a pause. Peter boils

Peter Did you?

Mike Did I?

Grigore Yes!

Peter You didn't!

Mike Apparently.

Peter Of all the back-stabbing . . .! You low down, conniving little . . .!
Mike Hold on, Pete! It wasn't really me . . .!
Peter Oh no. Sorry.
Grigore Peter, iss mistake. I'm sure!
Peter We'll soon find out. (*He crosses to the phone*)
Mike Where are you going?
Peter Saudi Arabia, that's where I'm going.
Mike Now?
Peter As soon as I've rung David Goodram.
Mike But Peter. What if you can't?
Peter Can't?
Mike Go.
Peter No such word as can't!
Mike I'm not so sure.
Peter And if Goodram won't back down . . .
Mike Yes?
Peter Simple.
Mike What?
Peter I'll resign.
Mike Oh . . . AH! Now hold on a minute!
Peter No . . . there's a principle at stake here, Mike.
Mike There's more than a principle. There's half the marriages in New
    Malden!

Peter starts dialling furiously

Peter Now look Mike. Keep Jane out of here until I've got to the bottom of
    this! She'll freak if she hears.
Mike Peter. This could all be a misunderstanding!
Peter I don't think so. It's got a smell of truth about it. He's been behaving
    very oddly the last couple of days, that David Goodram fellow . . .
Mike But even if it is true, it doesn't matter.
Peter Doesn't matter?!
Mike No! You can't go, anyway . . . I mean . . .
Peter Can't go? What the hell are you talking about?! Jane has set her heart
    on it.
Mike I don't think she has.
Peter (*on the phone*) Oh, David? . . . Oh, Marjorie.
Mike Oh dear.

Peter wanders into the hall with the phone

Peter (*on the phone*) I need to speak to him urgently . . .
Mike (*looking at his cigar*) It really tastes very odd this.

*Peter continues his conversation, obviously leaving a message for David
Goodram to ring him back*

*Meanwhile, Jane, Stella and Polly come out of the kitchen. Mike rushes to
block their entrance and talks very loudly to drown the telephone conversation*

Mike You can't come in!
Jane What?
Mike You can't come in. Please wait in the kitchen!
Stella Mike? What are you up to?
Mike (*pointing at Grigore*) It's ... HIM!
Jane Grigore? What's happened now?
Mike Nothing's happened. He's just ... changing his trousers, that's all!
Jane Why?
Polly He hasn't ...!!
Mike No. Nothing like that. His are too tight for the bandages that's all!
Jane But he doesn't have to ...
Mike So we're giving him an old pair of Peter's. So if you don't mind ladies?
Jane Who's Peter on the phone to?
Mike Peter?
Jane Peter. My husband. Who's he on the phone to?
Mike He's ... er ... ordering some food ...!
Peter (*on the phone in the hall*) Just tell him Peter rang. Peter, that's it!
Mike Pizzas! Pizzas all round! OK? Jolly good! Now, off you go back in the kitchen.

Mike pushes Jane, Stella and Polly back in the kitchen and slams the door

Peter re-enters

Peter Damn!
Mike What did he say?
Peter He wasn't there. He's ringing back.
Mike After all that!

Jane enters with her eyes shut, feeling her way in front of her

Jane I'm not looking! I'm not looking! I just want the tea towel.

Mike looks round for the tea towel, grabs it and presses it into Jane's hand

Thank you.

Jane exits

Peter (*utterly confused*) What was all that about?
Grigore Petro! Petro! You must not get yourself all in a pudding about this. Iss mistake I'm sure!
Peter Well you may be right, Grigore, but if the Saudi posting is off, I expect to be told!

The hatch opens and Jane's, Stella's and Polly's faces appear ... a bit giggly

Girls Can we come in yet?
Peter Yes!
Mike (*slamming the hatch*) No!
Peter What?
Mike Grigore's trousers!
Peter What about them?

Mike We've got to change them!
Peter Have we?
Mike Yes!
Peter Whatever for? He hasn't wet them, has he?
Mike No, but ...
Peter What's got into you, Mike? Now look. Not a word of this to Jane ... understand?
Mike Yes, but ...
Peter Understand, Grigore. If there's any truth in what you say and I'm not going to Saudi, she be heartbroken. Not a word to my wife! She be very upsetee!
Mike But, Peter ...
Peter This is neither the time nor the place to be dropping bombs like that.
Grigore Bombs? I sink she is all my mistake!
Mike I sink she is!
Peter Nonsense. Just let's see what Goodram says when he rings ...
Mike Peter, Peter.
Peter What?
Mike Look ... just do me a favour, will you?
Peter Oh not now, Mike! I'm in the middle of a crisis!
Mike Listen. Go into the kitchen ... and tell your wife that this Saudi thing may be off.
Peter Are you completely off your head?!
Mike Just see what she says!
Peter What the hell is in those things you're smoking!
Polly
Stella } *(together, off)* Come on you lot!
Jane
Mike Peter! Listen to me ...!
Peter Don't you say a word! ... All right! Come in!

Mike despairs

Polly, Jane and Stella enter

Stella All done?
Peter What is?
Jane Grigore.
Peter Grigore?
Stella Yes. All changed now?

Peter looks baffled

Peter Into what exactly? A frog or something? You haven't changed, have you, Grigore? You're not mutating quietly on the sofa there, are you?
Grigore Vot?
Peter The girls think you've changed in some way!
Mike *(through the corner of his mouth)* He has!
Peter Has he?
Mike Yes! His trousers!

Peter Mutating trousers, how unusual!

Mike *We* changed them for him.

Peter You know it's extraordinary, but everytime I answer the telephone it's like entering a time warp. Something happens that I don't know about.

Stella Mike said we couldn't come in just now because Grigore was changing his trousers.

Peter Oh! . . . Ah! . . . *Those* trousers. Yes! I see . . . well it wasn't necessary in the end.

Jane Oh. Why not?

Peter It was only his drink.

Jane What was?

Peter What he'd spilled. He thought . . . well Mike and I thought and Grigore agreed . . . that the shock of hitting his head had led to *un petit accident.*

Polly That's concussion that is! I knew it! We should take him to the hospital.

Peter Don't be ridiculous, Polly!

Polly It is! If he thought he was when he wasn't, he obviously doesn't know whether he is or not.

Peter What?

Polly Relieving himself! He could have brain damage!

Mike Oh for goodness sake!

Peter Polly, it's time you went home.

Grigore Oh . . . no!

Peter Oh . . . yes!

Polly I'm not going back to that maniac!

Jane Polly, I think Peter's right.

Polly What about my pizza?

Peter Indeed! I should think it's done to a turn by now.

Polly Ooh good! Who's going to get it?

Peter You are, Polly, if you don't go home! Good bye.

Stella I think she means: who's going to collect the pizza.

Peter Oh . . . I see! Well now, there's a question to tax some of the greatest brains in Europe! Who is going to collect the pizzas? Welcome to another edition of *Mastermind.* This week we find ourselves in the historic and elegant University of New Malden. Our first contestant is Peter Harbottle and his specialized subject is pizzas. Your first question, Peter: Who is going to collect the pizzas? Pass! Second question: How did the pizzas currently being discussed at twenty-three, Key Hill Drive, New Malden, first orginate? Pass! Third question: Why did pizzas even enter the conversation in the first place? Pass! Fourth question: Why is it . . . Bleep! Bleep! I've started so I'll finish . . . Why is it that you haven't the foggiest idea what anyone is talking about? Pass! And at the end of that round, Mr Harbottle, you have scored no points! Thank you very much. I give up. Who's going to collect the pizzas?

Jane Peter?

Peter Yes, Jane?

Jane Why don't you sit down?
Peter Yes, Jane.

The phone rings

I'll get it.
Jane You sit down.

Jane pulls Peter back by his braces

Peter It's all right. It's for me.
Jane How do you know? You haven't even answered it yet.
Peter I can tell by the ring.
Jane Stop playing the fool and sit down.
Peter It's for me! It's for me, I tell you! (*Into phone*) Hullo? . . . yes? . . . Hold on . . . It's for Polly.
Jane Polly?
Polly Me?
Peter Your name's Polly, isn't it?
Polly Yes.
Peter Then it's for you.
Polly Who is it?
Peter How do *I* know?
Jane Well ask!
Peter Excuse me, but who are you? . . . (*Suddenly very serious*) Oh. I see. One moment . . . It's the one-legged gamekeeper.

There is a pause as everyone tries to take this in

Jane Don't be so stupid, Peter! Who is it?
Peter Donald.
Polly (*ducking under the table*) Aaaah!
Jane What are you doing, Polly?
Polly Sorry. Instant reflex. I can't speak to him.
Jane Oh, for goodness sake, Polly!
Polly I can't! He'll hit me!
Jane He can't hit you. He's the other end of a telephone.
Polly He'll spit then.
Peter Will somebody please tell me what to do with Donald?
Polly You speak to him, Jane!
Jane Me?
Peter Good idea! Come along, Jane.
Jane But I can't! It's none of my business.
Peter Polly is a guest in our house. That makes it your business. Now come on, Jane, jump to it.
Stella Yes, go on, Jane!
Mike You can do it, Janey!
Jane What shall I say?!
Peter You'll think of something. You always do.

So Jane rather coyly takes the phone, pointlessly tidying her hair as she does. She speaks so charmingly to Donald that it's almost flirtatious

Jane Hello? Donald ... Hullo! It's Jane Harbottle here ... Polly isn't available at the moment. Can I help at all? ... Yes, of course, I can take a message ... mmmmh ... yes ... mmmmh ... right, got that ... mmmmh ... mmmmh ...

Jane wanders into the hall with the phone

Peter hobbles back to the sofa

Jane continues to make meaningful noises on the phone in the hall

Polly Oh God! What's he saying?

Peter (*in an urgent whisper*) Shut up, Polly and listen to me ... all of you. Any minute now, I'm getting a call from David Goodram. It's absolutely imperative that Jane is out of the room when he rings.

Stella Whatever for?

Peter It's too complicated to explain.

Mike It's to do with the Saudi posting.

Grigore Saudi iss all my mistake.

Stella Saudi posting?

Polly Do they have Post Offices in Saudi?

Peter Shut up, Polly! Jane must not ... under any circumstances ... overhear my conversation.

Mike Peter, can I say something?

Peter What?

Mike I think you and Jane should have a chat.

Peter Excellent idea. I'll get my secretary to arrange it.

Stella Is there some doubt about you going to Saudi Arabia?

Peter Yes.

Stella Then so do I.

Peter So do you what?

Stella Think you and Jane should have a chat. I think we should all go home and leave you two to sort this out. Come along, Polly.

Grigore Oh no! My Polly!

Stella Mike, get your things.

Peter No! No! Wait! I'm depending on you to get Jane out of the way while I speak to David Goodram!

Stella (*taking Peter's hand*) Peter. My dear Peter. This evening's charade has gone on quite long enough. You and Jane are both adults and both capable of intelligent communication.

Peter I disagree.

Stella Well so do I. But even so, I think we should go. (*She kisses Peter*)

Peter No! Stella! ... Please! (*Holding on to Stella*)

Jane comes off the phone, and re-enters

Peter lets go of Stella's hand. He looks guilty

Polly What did he say?

Jane He seemed very repentant.

Polly Probably standing there now with armfuls of wet smelly cheese waiting for me to walk through the door. I'm not going over there.

Jane I think you're being very silly.
Peter I don't.
Jane Be quiet, Peter.
Polly Anyway, what about my pizza?
Peter Not again. I can't bear it.
Jane You'll just have to . . .
Peter On second thoughts, well remembered, Polly! Time we all had pizzas. Off you go, Jane, and get us all some food.
Stella I should think they've been given to someone else by now.
Peter What have?
Stella The pizzas.
Peter We haven't even ordered them yet. How can they be given to someone else?
Stella You ordered them earlier on.
Peter I didn't order any pizzas.
Stella Yes, you did. On the phone.
Peter Hullo, it's another time warp.
Mike (*through the corner of his mouth*) When the *girls* were in the *kitchen* . . . you ordered pizzas.

Peter looks blank

When you were *on the phone*!
Peter (*through the corner of his mouth*) Right! Right! . . . Ha! All coming back to me now!
Stella Anyway, it's far too late to go and collect them. Another time, perhaps. Good night everyone . . .!

Peter grabs Stella imploringly

Peter No! Jane? Go and collect the pizzas now please.
Jane Can't someone else go? Then I can stay and get everything . . .
Peter No.
Jane What about Stella? I'm sure she and Mike . . .
Peter She's staying with me.
Stella No, Peter. I think . . .
Jane Why . . . is Stella staying here with you?
Peter Why? . . . Why? . . . WHY? . . . look, never mind why. Just go and collect the pizzas.
Stella No, I'm sorry. I think it would be far better if Mike and I . . .
Peter Please Stella . . .? (*Flirting with her playfully*)
Stella Well I . . .
Peter For me? . . . Mmmmh? (*Stroking Stella*)
Stella Well I . . . well I . . . well I . . . (*Going all weak and silly*) Oh all right!
Peter (*relieved*) Thank you! You're an angel! (*He kisses Stella*) Off you go, Jane and get the pizzas please.
Polly Can I come?
Jane No, Polly. You're going back to Donald.
Polly I am not. Not on my own.
Jane (*playing an ace*) Then . . . Peter will have to go with you.

Peter I can't do that.
Jane Oh? And why not, pray?
Peter I'm expecting a phone call.
Jane Really? Who from?
Peter Father Christmas. Look, it doesn't matter who from. I'm not taking Polly.
Jane I see.
Peter I'm not going to sit in Polly's front room and have clods of Camembert thrown at me.
Jane No. Quite. Then it looks as though I shall have to take you, Polly, doesn't it? And seeing as Peter and Stella are otherwise engaged, Mike will have to get the pizzas.
Polly Aaaaah!
Stella Polly! Don't do that!
Jane What is it?
Polly He's dead!
Peter What?
Polly Grigore! I knew it was brain damage!

They all gather round Grigore who lies on the sofa, eyes closed and mouth wide open. They all peer down at him. He suddenly takes one of those sharp intakes of breath accompanied by a grotesque snore. All reel back at another wave of garlic breath

Jane He's fallen asleep, that's all. What shall we do with him?
Polly He might be in a coma.
Peter Mike and I'll have to carry him upstairs.
Stella Why don't you just leave him?
Polly I think we should call an ambulance.
Peter Do shut up, Polly! Come on, Mike, give me a hand.

Mike and Peter gently try to lift Grigore out of the armchair. They succeed for a moment but then topple over onto the sofa and Grigore's embrace. Mike and Peter are trapped

Grigore Oooh, my pretty Polly! (*He smacks Peter's behind*)
Peter It's all right, Grigore. It's only us.
Grigore Sing for me! Sing for me my little song bird!
Peter I'm suffocating here!
Mike Get your head under his armpit!
Peter Get your own head under his armpit!
Mike I have! ... Pooh! Blimey! He's like a walking Wimpy Bar! Let go, Grigore!
Grigore I'll never let you go! Polly! You have the face of Diana and ... (*He grabs Peter's buttock*) the cheeks of Apollo!
Peter The cheeks of Apollo?! Get off, Grigore! OK, Mike. Let's try and get him on his feet. When I say three. One ... two ... three!

They succeed and begin to make slow progress towards the door

Grigore Sing for me! I no hear you, my little dove!

Mike Sing, Polly, for God's sake!
Polly Doves don't sing, they coo.
Peter Then coo, woman!
Polly I don't know how to coo!
Grigore Polly! Polly! Where are you?!
Peter Give him a blast of the madrigal ... anything to let him know you're here!

Polly begins to sing

Grigore Aaah! That's better ... That is what I like ...!

Mike, Polly, Peter and Grigore make steady progress out of the room, into the hall and presumably up the stairs. Polly's voice and Grigore's attendant appreciation fades into the distance

Jane and Stella are alone. Jane is very frosty

Stella Jane, listen to me. You must talk to Peter.
Jane This may come as rather a surprise to you, Stella, but that is exactly what I have been trying to do since seven o'clock this evening.
Stella I know and it's partly my fault. But you *must* speak to him as soon as you've sorted Polly out. We won't be here.
Jane Really? It won't be the same without you.
Stella I'm serious, Jane. Tell him about the baby. We'll give you plenty of time.
Jane Before what?
Stella Before we get back with the pizzas.
Jane I see. I thought you were staying here with Peter.
Stella Oh, ignore all that. I'm going with Mike.
Jane Most considerate. You're sure it's no trouble?
Stella Look. I'm not saying anything ...
Jane There's something I've been meaning to say to you, Stella.
Stella Yes, darling. What?
Jane This thing with Peter ... it's getting a little out of hand.
Stella You're telling me! I wish to goodness the two of you would sit down and *talk* to each other!
Jane I don't mean that, Stella. I mean the other thing.
Stella What other thing?
Jane The other thing we talked about this afternoon.
Stella We talked about lots of things.
Jane Oh, you know ...!
Stella No! I don't know! What?
Jane The way you flirt with him.
Stella Flirt? Me? With who?
Jane Peter! You do, Stella ... it's no use denying it. I told you he has always had a bit of a thing about you. I wish I'd never mentioned it now, but you're always playing up to it.

Stella is speechless

Stella (*not knowing whether to laugh or explode*) Jane! ... I'm ... I'm ... I don't know what I am ... I'm ...!

Jane Well you're slightly overdoing it for a start. All that nurse in residence stuff earlier on. And you cuddling up to him on the sofa.

Stella But that was ...

Jane And then, when you were giving your rendering of Kate, the gypsy, you danced all over him.

Stella Danced all over him?

Jane Caressing his leg.

Stella Caressing his leg? You're not at all well, Jane ...!

Jane Yes. You did a kind of thing with your hips.

Stella A thing?

Jane Yes.

Stella What kind of thing?

Jane A thing ... you know!

Stella I haven't the faintest idea! Show me please?

Jane Well ... it was ... it was ... (*She illustrates with a ridiculous wiggle of her hips*) ... I don't like it, Stella! Please don't do it anymore.

Stella We were trying to get you out of a sticky situation, if you can remember that far back!

Jane Well I'm grateful for that, but I'd appreciate it if you didn't make up to him anymore.

Peter, Mike and Polly re-enter. The room is heavy with tension between Stella and Jane

Peter That's that done.

There is a pause

Mike All right, Stella?

Stella Yes, thank you.

Jane Right. Well ... Polly and I had better be off then. Come along, Polly.

Peter Good luck, Poll. And remember ... entering by the narrow door is never easy ... especially when there's a four course meal coming straight for you!

Polly sees this as her dramatic moment. She goes to Peter melodramatically and nestles in his arms

Polly Oh Peter! Dear Peter!

Peter Ssh! Ssh! ... I know.

Polly Can I say something before I go?

Peter Of course.

Polly I've always ...

Peter Always what, mmmh?

Polly I've always had a bit of a thing about you!

Jane and Stella explode. Jane marches Polly to the front door

Stella⎫ *(together, variously)*⎧ Oh for goodness sake, girl!
Jane ⎭   ⎨ I think I may get violent in a minute! . . . Come
                                     ⎩ on!

Jane and Polly exit, and the door slams

Mike She really is very odd that girl.
Stella Peter. I don't think I can stand much more of this, so I'm going to
stick my neck out and tell you something . . .

The phone rings

Peter David Goodram! Right on the button!
Stella Oh, what's the use? Come on Mike! . . . MIKE!

*Mike has been tentatively trying out a few Greek dance steps quietly in the
corner. He giggles to himself. Peter and Stella are mesmerized for a brief
moment*

What the hell d'you think you're doing?
Mike Sorry. I was just . . . I thought you were staying here with Peter . . .
Stella *(marching Mike to the hall)* Don't you start, for heaven's sake! Let's
go and get these blasted pizzas.
Mike *(as they go)* But I don't understand . . .!
Stella Don't argue with me you stupid little man!
Mike Don't call me a stupid little man!

Mike and Stella exit, arguing. The door slams

Peter *(picking up the phone)* Hullo? David? Yes! . . . Yes! . . . Yes! . . .
Yes! . . . Yes! . . . Yes. Awfully good of you to ring back. I wonder if you
could clear up a slight misunderstanding this end . . .

*Peter wanders into the hall with the phone. His voice fades as he goes out of
sight and music fades up*

*After a moment Peter reappears from the kitchen with an apron on. It is
about ten minutes later. Peter is pacing in and out of the kitchen,
reminiscent of Jane in Act I. He looks nervous and is drying up pots and
pans*

Peter Jane, darling . . . I know you've had your heart set on Saudi, I know it
would be an exciting place to go but . . . I . . . No! That isn't the right way
to tell her, Peter.

Peter goes into the kitchen and appears at the hatch

Right, Jane. Saudi . . . is . . . off! OK? . . . Oh hell!

Peter mutters on to himself in the kitchen

*We hear keys turning in the front door and Jane enters. Peter doesn't hear
her. Jane stops and listens*

Darling! . . . I care about you so much . . . and we've got so many friends
here . . . I mean—Stella. I love you . . . and I . . .

Jane (*a violent whisper*) Stella!

Peter I only want to do what's best, and you'd be losing such a good friend. I just think it's wrong . . . (*Seeing Jane*) Hi, Jane. Anyway, what I'm trying to say darling . . . JANE! (*He suddenly looks guilt-ridden. He starts polishing a glass furiously through the hatch*)

Jane I knew it!

Peter Knew what?

Jane You and Stella.

Peter Me and Stella? What about me and Stella?

Jane (*mimicking him*) "What about me and Stella?" What the hell have you two been up to?

Peter Nothing.

Jane Don't lie to me, Peter! I know when you're lying!

Peter Well . . .

Jane All that nonsense about the pizzas . . . what's going on?

Peter Damn! I knew you'd suspect something.

Jane Behind my back like a couple of sixth formers. Ha! You must think I'm really dim!

Peter Jane, it wasn't behind your back exactly, I just . . .

Jane You're right! You're dead right! It's out in the bloody open now!

Peter Is it? Oh hell!

Peter comes into the living-room and closes the hatch

I didn't want you to find out from anyone else. I wanted to tell you myself.

Jane How very considerate.

Peter Stella, presumably?

Jane Stella, what?

Peter Who told you.

Jane Who else! Devious little . . .!

Peter Now come on, Jane. Don't be too hard on her. She was all for getting it out in the open.

Jane I'll bet she was!

Peter But I had to make sure, you see . . . before telling you myself. Darling, I am sorry. You must be so disappointed.

Jane Disappointed? No . . . not really. Surprised, perhaps. Shocked, a little . . . and even slightly nauseous. But now your grubby little secret's out . . .

Peter OK. Cards on the table. Let me explain.

Jane Certainly. Explain away!

Peter I only found out this evening.

Jane Ha!

Peter Try not to be angry, Jane. Quite honestly, it was Mike's fault, he . . .

Jane Oh yes! That's it! Blame it all on duvet-belly! Poor fool . . . you wait 'til he hears what Stella's been . . .

Peter Oh, Mike knows already.

Jane Mike knows?

Peter Oh yes. Well, to be honest he's had more to do with this than Stella.

Jane I don't follow.
Peter Well . . . it's silly really. It's much less complicated than it sounds . . .
the fact is, this whole thing started with . . . You're not going to believe
this . . .
Jane Try me.
Peter Well, this whole thing started with Mike and me on the sofa.
Jane You and Mike?
Peter Yes.
Jane You're right. I don't believe it.
Peter We were chatting away about this and that . . .
Jane On the sofa?
Peter On the sofa. Yes. I just said we were on the sofa . . . and one thing led
to another . . .
Jane You mean . . .?
Peter It was pointless trying to cover it up. You were bound to find out
sooner or later but . . . I needed to be sure. I should have come right out
and told you. I'm sorry.
Jane No, no. This can't be happening.
Peter Well, it's true, I'm afraid. There we were chatting away and every-
thing got a bit out of control.
Jane You and Mike.
Peter Me and Mike.
Jane On the sofa. On *our* sofa!
Peter Yes. Don't keep going on about the sofa. It couldn't matter less
where . . .
Jane Hell's teeth! Mike . . . of all people!
Peter I know. Ridiculous involving someone like him in a caper like that.
Jane And you!
Peter And Grigore, of course.
Jane GRIGORE!?
Peter He was the one that set the ball rolling. If he hadn't opened his big
mouth . . .
Jane I never liked the Greeks.
Peter Now, steady on, Jane. It wasn't his fault. He'd had a bang on the
head, a fair amount to drink and he just let something slip. Anyway, it all
snowballed from there, rather leaving me with my trousers down.
Jane Poor you.
Peter Yes. Well, there we are. These things happen. So that all led to the
misunderstanding between Mike and me about Grigore's trousers . . .
Jane How sweet.
Peter And it was then I decided to drag Stella in. Ha! She thinks I'm a bit
off the rails, you know? Dear Stella . . . I'm very fond of her, Jane . . . well
. . . I'm fond of them both really.
Jane So it would seem. A merry little *menage à trois*.
Peter They're terribly anxious for us to talk this through.
Jane Are they?
Peter Yes. So let me give it to you straight.
Jane From what you tell me there's nothing straight about it!

Peter Well I admit the road has been a little twisted.

Jane Bent would be more descriptive.

Peter Bent, twisted, whatever . . . let me tell you the situation.

Jane Oh do! Do! Or better still . . . Stella can tell me herself.

Peter Stella?!

Jane Yes! (*Banging on the kitchen hatch*) . . . Come on, Gypsy Rose Kate! Out you come!

Peter Stella isn't in here, Jane. She's fetching pizzas!

Jane I see. Having got this far, you now expect me to believe that Stella wasn't in there with you?

Peter I don't expect anything. I'm telling you. She . . .!

Jane Let me get this clear. Stella isn't here, but you are . . .

Peter Well, I'm beginning to wonder now . . .!

Jane All right. Let's try again. You and Mike found yourselves in the middle of this crazy affair . . .

Peter After Grigore had got me going on the sofa . . .

Jane Indeed. All thanks to Grigore.

Peter When he told me about David Goodram shifting his stance.

Jane Nicely put. DAVID GOODRAM? He's not in on this as well?

Peter Yes.

Jane Bloody hell! It's an epidemic!

Peter He's the cause of it all, quite honestly. If he had stuck to his guns and hadn't been so airy fairy, it would never have come up in the first place!

Jane Tut! Tut! Tut! Naughty old David Goodram!

Peter Well, quite! Jane, I am sorry . . . and listen, while we're on the subject of apologies, you're not to worry about the fine.

Jane Fine? . . . Peter? (*Alarmed*) What fine, please?

Peter The TV licence fine. What other fine is there?

Jane I wasn't sure but . . . for a moment here, I thought we were into soliciting.

Peter No, no. There won't be any need for solicitors. Anyway, it's fine about the fine.

Jane Fine is it?

Peter Fine. Really.

Jane Well, I don't find the fine fine at all. I find the fine anything but fine! Frankly, I wish they'd taken you off then and there . . . and put you away where you belong!

The front doorbell rings

Peter Damn! That'll be Stella and the pizzas.

Jane Sounds like a children's story. "Stella and the Pizzas"—an exciting bedtime adventure . . . for twisted kids!

The bell rings again more urgently

Aren't you going to answer it?

Peter Can't you?

Jane No way! I want to watch. I want to see how good you are at charades!

Peter hobbles to the front door. He disappears for a second and then lurches back into view with Stella in his arms. She is very upset

Peter Stella!

Stella Oh Peter! . . . Jane!

Jane Stella! What a surprise! How did you manage it? Through the back door and round the front?

Stella Mike and I have had the most awful row!

Jane Very good! Very good!

Peter Do shut up, Jane! What was the row about, Stella?

Stella It was silly really. All about this evening and us getting involved . . .

Jane Oh how silly.

Stella I'm sorry to rush back so soon. Have you told Jane, by the way?

Peter Well, sort of . . .

Jane Yes! Yes! All sorted out now. All out in the open!

Stella Oh good. At least something has come out of this ridiculous mess.

Jane Yes. Peter has.

Stella Peter has what?

Jane Come out . . . Oh, never mind. So, Stella. Where are the pizzas?

Stella Mike's bringing them.

Jane I see.

Stella What's left of them. He decided to throw one at me.

Jane Just the one?

Stella Yes.

Jane Didn't do much damage.

Stella No. He missed altogether. Flew straight passed me and hit a policeman coming round the corner.

Peter Grief! Where's Mike now?

Stella Still trying to make amends, I imagine. Last I saw, he was peeling anchovies off the bewildered bobby's helmet.

Peter Come and sit down, Stella. I'm sure it'll all blow over.

Jane Oh yes, bound to! Blow over like a handful of fairy dust.

Peter Jane, you're not being very sympathetic.

Jane Oh. Aren't I? Sorry! What shall I do? I know! I'll ring up David Goodram and ask him if he'll pop on his nurse's uniform and come over!

Stella David Goodram? Oh yes, Mike told me how he fitted in.

Jane Did he, by Jove.

Stella You mustn't be bitter, Jane.

Jane Bitter? Me? No! Tart would be accurate, I think . . . like you!

Peter Jane! What are you saying!?

Jane Sorry! Was that a little strong? Have I upset your Stellybum's dinky little feelings?

Stella Please, Jane! Let's not go into all that again. I was hoping to find you two reconciled and enjoying the fact that all the misunderstandings were over.

Jane You're absolutely right, Stella. There are no misunderstandings now. Definitely not! It's all quite clear and it goes something like this: I've got a best friend who's A over T over my flexible husband who's AC/DC with her husband, his boss and the gay Greek in a drunken stupor upstairs . . .

The doorbell rings

. . . Excuse me, I think that's the door.

Jane skips to open the front door

Stella What's she talking about?
Peter I've no idea.
Jane (*off*) Hullo sailor!
Mike (*off*) Is Stella here?
Jane She certainly is.

Mike enters with five pizza boxes

Mike Stella? Stella! I'm sorry, darling! It was so stupid of me! All my fault!
Stella No. It was my fault. Anyway . . . at least you haven't been arrested, that's something.
Jane Early days. Give him time.
Mike Actually, he soon saw the funny side of it—poor old bobby. We had a bit of a chat, the law and me, and to show there were no hard feelings I slipped him one of Grigore's funny cigarillo things!
Stella Oh, well done you!
Mike Said he wasn't allowed to smoke it on duty so he'd keep it for later.
Stella Well I'm sure he appreciated it.
Mike As matter of fact . . . I gave him the whole box. Told him to hand them round to his colleagues at the nick.
Peter Sounds as though you handled yourself pretty well, Mike.
Mike Well . . . you know. "Think on your feet"; that's my motto.
Stella Anyway . . . sorry Pugwash.
Mike That's all right.
Stella Friends?
Mike Friends.

Mike and Stella hug

Jane Aaah! Isn't that touching. I'm touched, Peter. Aren't you?
Peter Mmmh? Oh. Yes.
Jane Don't you want to join in?
Peter Join in what?
Jane The touching bit.
Peter Oh . . . yes . . . all right.

Peter goes to embrace Jane. They hug. Jane suddenly knees Peter in the groin

Uuurgh!
Jane Not me! Them!
Peter Jane? What . . .?
Jane Right . . . would you like to lay the table, Peter?
Peter Lay the table?

Jane Yes. You seem to have laid everything else. (*Camp and lispy*) What have you done with the pizzas, Mike?

Jane goes out to the kitchen

Mike (*to Peter*) What's been going on?
Peter I'm not sure.

Jane re-enters with plates

Jane What's been going on, my dear, is that the worms have been crawling out of the woodwork! (*She dumps plates noisily on the table*)
Mike Really?
Jane Yes. Really.

Jane exits to the kitchen again

Mike Rentokil's supposed to be very good . . .
Stella (*urgently*) Peter, there's something wrong here. Why is Jane taking this all so badly?
Peter Well, it's understandable. She's disappointed . . .
Stella But she shouldn't be.
Peter Why not? After all, she had her heart . . .
Mike No! There's a reason!
Peter Reason for what?
Stella A reason why she shouldn't be disappointed!
Peter Sorry. I'm lost.
Stella What did you and Jane actually talk about when we were out?
Peter Well . . . I told her . . .

Jane re-enters with more plates and crockery. She bangs them down

Jane? What are you doing?
Jane Getting out the china.
Peter That's our best dinner service.
Jane They're our best friends.

Jane exits again to the kitchen

Mike Look. Peter, old chap (*putting his arm affectionately round Peter's shoulder*) I don't want to put my foot in it here, but when Stella and I were out throwing pizzas at each other, did you and Jane actually talk about this Saudi business?
Peter Yes! . . . I think so.
Stella And what was her reaction?

Jane enters with cups and saucers. She takes in the scene of Mike with his arm round Peter. She dumps her load of crockery on the table, growls maniacally and exits to the kitchen

Peter Jane! What the hell are you doing?

Jane bangs about in the kitchen even more. Stella takes Peter's hand earnestly and warmly

Stella (*with deep concern*) Peter. You must sort this thing out! There's obviously still some confusion. So I think Mike and I should just go. (*Kissing Peter*) Goodnight.

Jane re-enters and takes in the scene of Stella clutching Peter's hand and kissing him. Jane's eyes burn across the room, she dumps her load of even more crockery on the table, squeals maniacally and runs into the kitchen

Peter Jane! (*To Mike and Stella*) Look, can you see yourselves out? I'll go and talk to her right away. (*He makes a determined start towards the kitchen but his ankle stops him*) OW! . . . This bloody ankle! . . .

Peter staggers. Mike manages to catch him from falling over

Mike OK, OK, old chap! Take it easy!
Peter It hurts, it really hurts . . .!
Stella (*getting down on her knees to look*) Here, let me look at it a moment . . .

Jane re-enters to see Mike supporting Peter almost in an embrace and Stella kneeling at Peter's feet apparently kissing his ankle. Jane's eyes roll as she bangs her final load of crockery down on the table. The table is full

Jane Right! Come along, children. (*Clapping her hands like a mad schoolmistress*) Food and cabaret time!
Stella Jane, Peter's ankle looks really swollen . . .
Jane Help yourself to pizza everyone!
Peter Jane, what's going on? And why is all that valuable china spread across the table?
Jane We need plates to eat off, don't we?
Peter Yes, but you've got the complete service out!
Jane I know.
Peter Jane, can we talk?
Mike Stella and I are leaving. Come along, Stella.
Jane Do you want a plate to eat your pizza off, Peter?
Peter What? Yes. Look Jane . . .
Stella We'll see you two tomorrow.
Jane Here! Catch! (*She tosses a dinner plate across at Peter on the sofa*)
Peter What the blazes . . .!

Peter reaches for it. Mike and Stella also. All three end up in a heap on the sofa

Jane Isn't that nice? All cuddled up together on the sofa. Anyone else, plate?
Peter
Stella } (*together*) NO!
Mike
Peter Jane! What the devil's got into you?! That's incredibly valuable that china! It belonged to my grandparents!
Jane (*fondling another plate*) I know. The detail round the edge here is amazing.

Peter It's irreplacable. So stop playing the fool.
Stella Mike and I are going now, Jane. All right? ... Do as Peter says and
put all that china away. Put the kettle on ...
Jane Teach me to dance.
Stella Pardon?
Jane (*in a rich deep Greek voice*) "To dance?" ... Alan Bates and Anthony
Quinn, on the beach in *Zorba*. "You want to dance?!"
Stella Come along, Mike. I'll ring you in the morning, Jane.
Jane "Yes" ... Alan Bates, again ... "Like you!"
Peter Jane, I don't know what this is all in aid of but ...
Jane (*suddenly grabbing a second plate and dramatically holding it above her
head*) WATCH!
Peter Oh, good grief!
Jane (*beginning to sing* Zorba's *tune*) Darant! ... tish! Boom! Tish! ...
Peter Jane! What the hell do you think you're doing?
Jane Darant! Tish! Boom! Tish! ... Darant! tish!
Peter Put those plates down ... at once!
Jane Darant! ... Certainly ...

*In perfect rhythm with the tune and her slow dance, Jane tosses plates in the air
which Mike and Stella catch*

... Tish! Boom! Tish! (*etc*) ...
Peter Are you out of your mind?
Stella Jane, this is all very foolish ...!

*Jane picks up another two plates and begins to speed up her dance as in the
original*

Jane This is when he started to speed up. I loved this bit ... Darant-di-da-
dum-di-dida! Darant! ... (*etc*) ...

*As she accelerates Jane tosses a series of plates at Peter in quick succession.
He catches them all*

Jane Very good!
Peter Jane! You are to stop this ... RIGHT NOW! Come on, you two!
Help me stop her!

*Mike, Stella and Peter converge on Jane. She coolly grabs a whole pile of
dinner plates and holds them at bay*

Peter You'll regret this, Jane. I mean it.
Stella Do as he says, Jane ... please?
Mike Come on Janey ... put the plates down before something gets
broken. (*Approaching Jane slowly*) Better still, give them to me ...

Jane holds the pile above her head

... Come on ... no one's going to hurt you ... just hand me the plates ...
that's it ... come on ...

Peter (*angrily*) Jane! Do as Mike says ... NOW!

Jane simply removes her grip of the pile and walks away

Mike Oh God! (*He catches the pile before it hits the floor*)
Peter (*losing control*) JANE! ARE YOU COMPLETELY OUT OF
YOUR HEAD?

*Jane is unmoved and sings on. She appears from the table with arms
outstretched and plates balanced on the palms of each hand. She also has a
vegetable dish on her head. She dances nimbly round the room as she sings and
taunts the others. She passes her hands over their heads. They cannot catch her*

(*Hobbling after her*) You stupid woman! Give me those plates!
Stella Do stop, Jane! Please!
Mike Come on Jane! Enough's enough!

*Jane stretches her arms wide. Clearly she is going to smash the plates against
each other. At the critical moment, Peter grabs one plate, Stella the other and
Mike removes the vegetable dish from behind. Jane returns to the table. The
others hang on to the furniture, exhausted and convinced Jane has had enough.
Jane starts up again*

Jane Darant! ...

*In quick succession Jane throws Mike, Stella and Peter a coffee cup each
which they all catch. Then a saucer, which they all catch. They now all have
both hands full. Jane taunts Mike and Stella with another cup. She smiles at
Peter*

Peter No Jane! ... NO!

*Peter, with no hands free to catch anything, pleads with her. Jane tosses the
cup high in the air. Peter quickly puts the cup in his hand on the saucer in the
other and catches the flying cup*

JANE! YOU'RE INSANE!

*Jane, angered by this defeat, grabs the whole tray of crockery. She raises it up
over her head ... once, as the others sway in anticipation of her throwing it ...
twice, as she gets up a rhythm ... and the third time, when it would seem all is
lost ...*

Grigore enters, grabbing the tray out of Jane's hands

Grigore I sorry! I fall asleep! ... Come! We dance!
Mike ⎞ (*together*) OH GOD!
Stella ⎠
Peter No Grigore! NO!

*Grigore pirhouettes with the tray above his head. In desperation, Mike tackles
him round the waist, bulldozing him into the sofa. Grigore falls backwards over
the arm. Peter grabs the tray as Grigore goes over, but then trips, thrusting the
tray at Stella who catches it just before it hits the ground*

Polly enters in a PVC mac and bonnet. She is covered in food

Polly He's gone! Donald's left!

Grigore (*from under Mike who is sitting on him on the sofa*) Polly! My Polly!

A momentary pause. Polly takes in the scene and the others are speechless from exhaustion. Stella suddenly snaps and takes control

Stella Right. No one speak. I want paper, pens and envelopes.
Peter Stella. This is no time to play consequences.
Stella Quickly. Where are they?
Peter Stella . . .
Stella Answer me!
Peter Over there in the drawer.
Stella Get them!
Peter What for?
Stella Don't argue!
Peter Stella . . .!
Stella Do as you're told!

Peter wearily obeys. Stella takes Jane forcefully by the arm and sits her at the dining-table

Over here, you! . . . Sit!
Jane Get your hands off . . .!
Stella Silence! If you speak you'll be put in the corner!
Mike Stella, what are you doing?
Stella Unravelling this mess. Gather up the crockery, Mike . . . Peter! Will you hurry up!
Peter All right! I'm coming!
Polly What's going on?
Stella Have you got a spare room, Polly?
Peter Yes. It's between her ears.
Stella Shut up, you! Have you, Polly?
Polly Yes but . . .
Stella Right. Grigore, get your bags.
Grigore Bags?
Stella Get them for him, Polly.

Polly exits upstairs

Peter hobbles over with pens, paper and envelopes

Peter What's this all . . .?

Stella snatches the paper out of Peter's hands

Stella Sit! . . .

Peter sits next to Jane

Not there! (*Grabbing Peter by the arm*)
Peter Ow! Look Stella . . .!
Stella Opposite her! . . . I don't want any cheating.
Jane I'm not doing it! Whatever it is, I'm not doing it!
Stella Oh, yes you are. Now then. (*Distributing paper etc*) Pen, pen. Paper, paper. Envelope, envelope.

Peter What's happening?

Stella Five lines maximum. Two minutes in which to do it.

Peter Do what, for heaven's sake?

Stella You each write down what you've both been trying to tell each other this evening.

Jane ⎫ *(together)*⎧ I am not!
Peter ⎭   ⎩ Oh, look ...!

Stella Don't argue!

Jane I already know what flexible Fred here's been trying to tell me!

Stella You don't. I don't know what you *thought* he was telling you but it wasn't what *I* know, and *(pointing to the others)* he knows and *she* knows and half of bloody London know! Whatever it was, it wasn't what he was suppose to be telling you! Now, do it!

Jane But ...

Stella DO IT!

Like children doing an exam, Jane and Peter silently commence writing. They guard their paper from the other's view

Ready Mike?

Mike What shall I do with the pizzas?

Stella Wear them, for all I care. Ready Polly?

Polly comes downstairs with Grigore's bags

Polly Think so.

Grigore What we do? We go jumpy, jumpy now, Mike?

Mike No, Grigore! We go home ... to beddy, beddy!

Grigore But where?

Stella With Polly, Polly.

Grigore *(eyes lighting up)* Aaah! Yes!

Stella No! I didn't mean that! ... You'd better behave, Grigore ...

Peter He can do what he likes, Stella. He has diplomatic immunity!

Stella Get on with your work! And listen to me, Peter. You too, Jane. When you've finished writing you put your letters in the envelopes and seal them. Understand?

Peter ⎫ *(together)* Yes Stella.
Jane ⎭

Stella You then go upstairs and get ready for bed. Understand?

Peter ⎫ *(together)* Yes Stella.
Jane ⎭

Stella Once you're in bed, you may open the envelopes ... and read. Is that understood?

Peter ⎫ *(together)* Yes Stella.
Jane ⎭

Stella Right. Say good night to Peter and Jane, everyone.

Peter ⎫ *(together)* Goodnight to Peter and Jane, everyone.
Jane ⎭

Stella looks at them pitifully and starts ushering the others out

Peter Stella?
Stella What?
Peter Does "disappointed" have two "s"s or one?
Stella Oh, for goodness sake! ... Come on, you lot—out! ... OUT!

Stella, Mike, Grigore and Polly exit noisily, slamming the door

There is a moment's silence. Peter and Jane spontaneously poke their tongues out in the direction of Stella's exit. They look back at each other across the table, realizing they are finally alone. They both lick their envelopes and seal them

There is a pause. They eye each other cautiously

Peter Good 'ere, innit?
Jane Terrific. Laugh a minute.

There is a pause

Peter This is ridiculous.
Jane It's worse than ridiculous. It's pathetic.
Peter Jane?
Jane I'm not talking to you.
Peter What's happening to us?
Jane Huh.
Peter What does that mean—"huh"?
Jane Huh! Huh! Roughly translated, it means, "You tell me".
Peter I don't know ... I really don't.

Jane gets up and casually toys with one of the cups on the tray of crockery

Jane? What are you doing?
Jane It's all right! ... I was just going to put the tray on the side. Never knew you could catch so well.
Peter Neither did I. You must have been out of your mind!
Jane Who cares? It's insured, anyway.
Peter Only just.
Jane What do you mean, only just. Either it is or it isn't.
Peter I only renewed the premium last month.
Jane (*picking up the tray*) That's all right then ... what premium?
Peter I left it on the hall table with the TV licence ... Oh, my God.

Jane freezes mid-step in the middle of the room with the tray in her hands. She starts to tremble

Peter Jane!
Jane What shall I do with it?
Peter Just put it down!
Jane Where?
Peter On the floor!
Jane I can't move!
Peter Put it down, woman!
Jane It's heavy!

Peter Jane!
Jane Quickly! My hand's slipping!
Peter (*hobbling over to her*) Oh God! . . . Here, give it to me! . . .
Jane Got it?
Peter Gently, gently!
Jane Have you got it, Peter?
Peter Yes! If you'll . . . just . . . let go . . . LET GO, JANE!

Jane lets go. The tray drops about two feet

Peter }
Jane } (*together*) Aaah!

Peter manages to secure his grip

Jane Here! Put it in the hatch!
Peter (*hobbling over with the tray*) Clear some space, then!
Jane I am, I am!

Together they place the tray in the hatch. They stand back and look at it like an unexploded bomb

Peter Now, come away from it, Jane . . . Right away!
Jane All right! I am! . . . How much is it worth, anyway?
Peter I dunno. Hundreds. The stupid thing is . . . I loathe it.
Jane So do I.
Peter Can't stand the stuff.
Jane Why didn't you say before?
Peter Why didn't *you*?
Jane I thought you'd be angry.
Peter I thought you'd be upset.
Jane Five years of pretending.
Peter Par for the course, I'd say. Jane, I'm exhausted.
Jane So am I. Let's go to bed.
Peter Here's your letter.
Jane Here's yours.

They exchange envelopes

So . . . it's disappointing, is it?
Peter Yep.
Jane Very disappointing?
Peter Yep.
Jane Good.
Peter Good?
Jane Yes, 'cause so is mine.
Peter Right. Fine. Sounds as though we're in for a pretty depressing night, one way and another. I'll tell you one thing, we're not discussing any of it tonight. It's far too late. Agreed?
Jane Agreed. Supposing we can't sleep, though?
Peter What do you mean?
Jane Well . . . we can't just lie there seething away in the dark.
Peter True, true.

Jane So what do we do?
Peter We club each other unconscious. Now, off you go.
Jane Aren't you coming?
Peter I'll be up in a minute. I'll just switch everything out.
Jane You won't ... open yours, will you?
Peter Don't be childish! ... go on.
Jane Right. (*She begins going upstairs*)
Peter And don't you dare look at yours, either!
Jane Don't be so stupid, Peter!

Jane exits upstairs

Peter hobbles into the kitchen and reappears at the hatch. He puts his letter down to pick up the tray of crockery. He hesitates. He looks through the hatch into the living-room to check that Jane has gone. He wrestles with himself for a moment and finally yields to temptation. He carefully peels open the envelope, takes out the letter and reads. A look of sudden revelation creeps over his face. He understands but he hasn't taken in the information

Peter Oh! I see! Which is why ... and when ... Of course! God, I am slow sometimes ... I must be getting old ...! (*He puts the letter down. He chuckles to himself and mutters about how slow he has been to understand. As he does, he picks up the tray of crockery and vanishes from the hatch*)

There is a pause a sudden, terrifying and ugly crash of breaking crockery is heard, then silence

Jane comes running down the stairs, joyfully brandishing her letter

Jane Peter ... Peter! (*She looks around but cannot see him*) Peter?

Jane looks in the hatch. At the same moment Peter pops up and they bang heads. In spite of the pain they both laugh

Jane runs round into the kitchen

Peter and Jane stand framed in the hatch

Peter You know what?
Jane What?
Peter I love you, Jane Harbottle.

They kiss. As they do, we hear police sirens approaching at speed. We hear squealing tyres as the cars screech to a halt nearby. Peter and Jane break off from their kiss

Jane Five years and I still hear trumpets.
Peter You know something else?
Jane What?
Peter (*looking around him on the floor*) I think I've cracked it.

They are about to kiss again when the doorbell rings urgently

Leave it. Whoever it is, they can wait.

As they are about to resume their kiss, they are stopped by a loud voice

Megaphoned Voice We know you're in there! Come out with your hands up! ... We have you completely surrounded ... This is the drug squad!

Peter and Jane slowly look out front. They peer through the hatch. Without saying a word they pull the hatch doors shut and disappear beneath them

The Lights fade to a Black-out

FURNITURE AND PROPERTY LIST

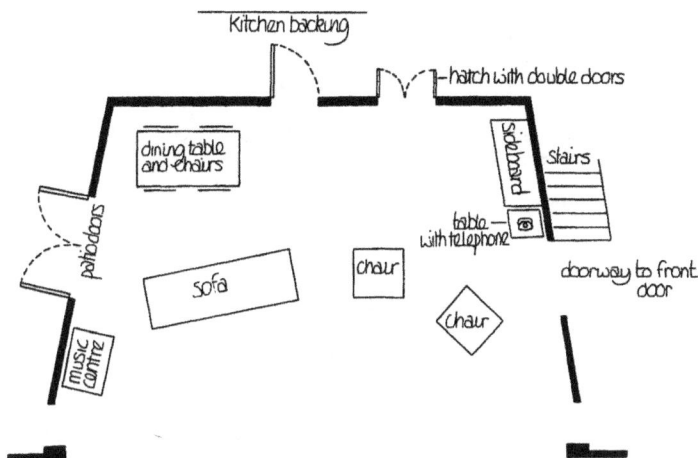

ACT I

On stage: Sofa with cushions
Coffee table. *On it:* paper knife
Two easy chairs
Small table with telephone
Dining-table and chairs
Sideboard. *In it:* china, candlesticks. *In a drawer:* bandage
Music centre: i.e. combined record player and cassette player

Off stage: Mug of tea **(Stella)**
Tablecloth and cutlery **(Jane)**
Crockery—two separate piles **(Jane)**
Electric mixer in kitchen, near hatch, with mixing bowl and fork or whisk
for beating contents **(Jane)**
Briefcase. *In it:* a file **(Peter)**
Two drinks in glasses **(Jane)**
Drink in glass **(Peter)**
Bottle of champagne **(Mike)**
Four champagne glasses **(Jane)**
Trifle (in **Polly's** hair)

Golf club **(Peter)**
Briefcase and carrier bag containing two large bottles of ouzo, a box of
    perfume, "special" cigar, cassette **(Grigore)**
Vacuum cleaner **(Jane)**

ACT II

On stage: The same furniture as Act I
            Tea towel on chair
            Paper, pens and envelopes in sideboard drawer

Off stage: Tray of drinks **(Mike)**
            Cigarillo **(Mike)**
            Pots and pans, glasses, tea towel **(Peter)**
            Five pizza boxes **(Mike)**
            Five separate piles of crockery, including plates, cups and saucers, large
               vegetable dish, and a tray **(Jane)**
            Food to cover **Polly's** PVC mackintosh and bonnet
            Bags **(Polly)**

LIGHTING PLOT

ACT I

Early evening

To open: Bright interior lighting, some light spilling through the patio doors; this spill fades very gradually throughout the act

Cue 1   **Jane:** "This is Jane Harbottle, News at Ten, New bloody
        Malden."   (Page 36)
        Black-out

ACT II

Evening

To open: Bright interior lighting

Cue 2   **Peter** and **Jane** close the hatch doors   (Page 64)
        Slow fade to black-out

EFFECTS PLOT

ACT I

Cue 1   **Jane** paces up and down the kitchen   (Page 6)
Keys turn in front door

Cue 2   **Jane:** "Well . . . there's a reason—you see—"   (Page 9)
Telephone rings

Cue 3   **Peter:** "What were you going to tell . . .?"   (Page 10)
Doorbell rings

Cue 4   **Peter:** ". . . pointing the wrong way, that's all . . . Ah!"   (Page 14)
Telephone rings

Cue 5   **Jane:** "Ooooooooooooaaaaaaaarrrgh!"   (Page 19)
Crash of breaking crockery

Cue 6   **Jane** slams the hatch in **Peter**'s face   (Page 20)
Doorbell rings

Cue 7   **Jane** dashes into the kitchen   (Page 21)
Bangs from kitchen

Cue 8   **Jane, Mike** and **Stella** head for the kitchen door   (Page 23)
Doorbell rings

Cue 9   **Jane:** "I think I'm going to scream."   (Page 24)
Telephone rings

Cue 10   **Jane** switches on the vacuum cleaner   (Page 34)
Vacuum cleaner starts

Cue 11   **Grigore** switches on the cassette player   (Page 34)
Loud Greek music plays

Cue 12   **Jane** switches off the vacuum cleaner   (Page 35)
Vacuum cleaner stops

Cue 13   **Peter** switches off the music   (Page 36)
Greek music stops; pause, then loud crash

ACT II

Cue 14   **Peter:** "Yes, Jane."   (Page 43)
Telephone rings

Cue 15   **Jane** and **Polly** exit   (Page 49)
Door slams

Cue 16   **Stella:** ". . . stick my neck out and tell you something."   (Page 49)
Telephone rings

Cue 17	**Mike** and **Stella**, exit, arguing *Door slams*	(Page 49)
Cue 18	**Peter** wanders into the hall with the phone *Music fades up*	(Page 49)
Cue 19	**Peter** enters from kitchen *Music fades down*	(Page 49)
Cue 20	**Peter** mutters to himself in the kitchen *Keys turn in front door*	(Page 49)
Cue 21	**Jane:** ". . . and put you away where you belong!" *Doorbell rings*	(Page 52)
Cue 22	**Jane:** "—for twisted kids!" *Doorbell rings, more urgently*	(Page 52)
Cue 23	**Jane:** ". . . the gay Greek in a drunken stupor upstairs." *Doorbell rings*	(Page 54)
Cue 24	**Peter:** "Jane! What the hell are you doing?" *Bangs from kitchen*	(Page 55)
Cue 25	**Stella**, **Mike**, **Grigore** and **Polly** exit *Door slams*	(Page 61)
Cue 26	**Peter** vanishes from the hatch *Loud crash of breaking crockery*	(Page 63)
Cue 27	**Peter** and **Jane** kiss *Police sirens approach at speed with squealing tyres and brakes*	(Page 63)
Cue 28	**Peter:** "I think I've cracked it." *Doorbell rings*	(Page 63)

MADE AND PRINTED IN GREAT BRITAIN BY
LATIMER TREND & COMPANY LTD, PLYMOUTH
MADE IN ENGLAND

www.ingramcontent.com/pod-product-compliance
Lightning Source LLC
LaVergne TN
LVHW051801080426
835511LV00018B/3378